Shaw, Savill & Albion Co.LTD

ZEALANDIA

by Marolyn Diver & Belinda Lansley

*Ancestral Journeys
of New Zealand
Series*

Thanks to the following people:

Lisa Duggan, for the Edward Evans diary
Peter and Francie Diver
David Dudfield

Dornie Publishing Company

Grasmere, Invercargill

www.dorniepublishing.tk

Original text © Marolyn Diver and Belinda Lansley 2014

Images © named individuals, institutions.

All rights reserved.

ISBN: 978-0-473-29013-9

Cover design by Strawberrymouse Designs

Printed and bound in Invercargill, New Zealand by Dornie Publishing.

This book is dedicated to

Peter Diver

CONTENTS

	Introduction	7
1.	The Ship	9
2.	Disastrous Voyages	33
3.	Thirty-Two Voyages	43
4.	Passenger Biographies	69
5.	Passenger Lists	85
	References	134

Introduction

This book was started by Marolyn Diver as she had ancestors on board, Richard Diver and Catherine Hegarty, but she quickly got bogged down with other amazing projects and it fell into her unfinished pile. I joined the writing team to help get it finished. So together we have made a book and it is finally off our computers and published!

I had heard a bit about the ship *Zealandia* having a vague family connection to the Griebel family who were onboard the ship in 1870. I find immigrant ships fascinating and now have a catalogue of ship books behind me. I've learnt to never say, "I write ship books," at a noisy party. People hear it incorrectly.

Marolyn and I hope that this book will be helpful to those researching their ancestral ship and provide some insight into the terrors of the sea and the amazing ship *Zealandia*!

Belinda Lansley

The Ship

Zealandia pictured in Port Charmers

The *Zealandia* was a three-masted, full-rigged clipper-built ship with an iron hull, built by C. Connell, Glasgow in 1869 for the newly formed shipping company of Shaw, Savill & Co. Originally christened *The New Zealandia*, its name later change to *Zealandia* would cause some speculation and rumour. To understand why these accusations were rife one had to return to the origins of its owners Robert Shaw and Walter Savill.

Five years earlier both Shaw and Savill were employed by the commercially prosperous shipping company, Willis, Gann & Co, who in 1858 built a clipper ship they named *Zealandia*. She was one of many ships employed by the Canterbury province to bring assisted immigrants to New Zealand from 1855-60. Following a pay dispute with Willis, Gann & Co, Savill left soon after the launch of the first *Zealandia* to start his own company, soon enticing Shaw to follow.

It was somewhat scandalous at the time, but the fact that one of the first ships Shaw and Savill had was rechristened *Zealandia* led to some speculation that it was a small dig at their former bosses. Willis, Gann & Co were obviously no longer in a financial state to rebut as shortly thereafter sold their *Zealandia* and her new owners changed its name.

The exact reason why Shaw and Savill "took" the name will never be known, but one theory was that Shaw himself had come up with the name *"Zealandia"* while working for Willis, Gann & Co and, not liking them having his "creation", decided to make a fresh start with his own once he saw Willis, Gann & Co's *Zealandia* was on the verge of being decommissioned.

Another, perhaps more likely theory, was that Shaw and Seville had left Willis, Gann & Co on good terms and that it was Willis, Gann & Co who "gave" them the name, as their *Zealandia* was soon to be sold.

Whatever the reason, the two ships named *Zealandia* have caused much confusion over the years for family historians searching for their ancestor's ship and getting the names confused. Indeed for many years genealogical researchers believed that they were one and the same vessel; with the Willis, Gann and Co. *Zealandia* simply being purchased by Shaw & Savill in 1869. However further research shows that both ships differed in dimensions, and their separate history's can be traced from start to finish.

Shaw, Savill & Co's prized *Zealandia* was a beautiful ship, specially designed for carrying passengers in relative comfort compared to most other immigration ships. Though hardly first class, small efforts had been made to make the horrible three month journey more bearable for all passengers. Her cabins were unusually large and well ventilated, with extra large portholes. She had custom designed cabins for families, and a large ladies saloon. This saloon was elaborately decorated and was often talked about on shore for its subtle decadence. The second cabin was situated on deck with were larger than usual and well lit berths. All these small changes and extra details were to give *Zealandia* her head start amongst the competitive shipping industry. The fresh ideas Shaw, Savill & Co brought to shipping became a catalyst for how sea travel was to change, leading the way to treating passengers more like people and less like stock.

Neither Robert Shaw nor Walter Savill could have suspected that Shaw, Savill & Co were to become one of the most well known and respected British Shipping Companies in the world. Sadly Robert Shaw died from a heart attack at the age of forty one on the 24th of November 1860, only two years after the company's founding, and he was replaced by James W. Temple who insisted that the name of Shaw be retained in the company title. In 1882 the company name changed to Shaw, Savill & Albion and the *Zealandia* was transferred into the new company.

The *Zealandia's* Interior

This beautiful ship had three hospitals on board, one in the starboard after cabin, for families; one in the midship deck house for single men; and one in the port after cabin for single women away from men on board.

The single women were berthed separately, some situated in the after part of the poop and some in the after part of the 'tween decks with a ladder way from there into the poop and then another ladder onto the poop deck. The Matron's cabin was on the port side in the poop and she would have kept a close eye on the single women to make sure no men came near and that the women behaved. The single men's compartment was in the fore part of the 'tween decks, the fore hatchway, fitted with a booby hatch being their ladder way.

There was a water closet and bath room which were on the starboard side of the ship. There was a dispensary on the port side of the main hatchway.

The Clipper Ship

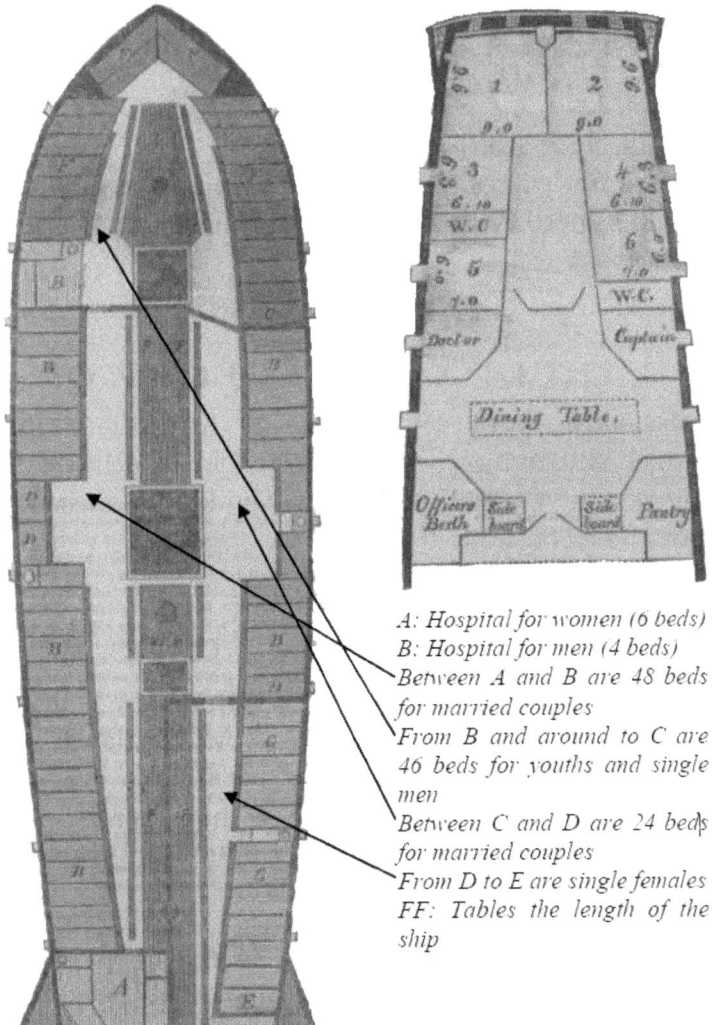

A: Hospital for women (6 beds)
B: Hospital for men (4 beds)
Between A and B are 48 beds for married couples
From B and around to C are 46 beds for youths and single men
Between C and D are 24 beds for married couples
From D to E are single females
FF: Tables the length of the ship

Plan of Emigrant Ship Between Decks (left) and Plan of Cabin Accommodation (right) (courtesy London Illustrated News)

Other Ships Called *Zealandia*

The following ships were owned by different companies and are not to be confused with the Shaw, Savill owned *Zealandia*!

Willis, Gann & Co.

Built in 1858 and captained by John Foster, *Zealandia* undertook 6 voyages to New Zealand. She served 9 years then was sold when Willis, Gann and Co sold up and left the shipping business.

HUDDART PARKER & CO

SS *Zealandia*, built 1910, was an Australian Cargo and passenger ship which was converted in to a troop transport during World War II. She was sunk by the Japanese at Darwin Harbour 19th February 1942.

THE ROYAL BRITSH NAVY

HMS *Zealandia* was a British battleship built 9 February 1904, she was originally christened "New Zealand" but was renamed *Zealandia* in 1911 and is the only Royal Navy ship to have had this name. After a short but lucrative career in World War I she was sold for scrap metal in 1921.

PACIFIC MAIL STEAMSHIP COMPANY.

R.M S.S *Zealandia* was a Pacific Mail steamer. Her maiden voyage was on 17 February 1876. She travelled mainly from San Francisco to Australia. She visited Lyttelton in 1876 and Auckland in 1877.

Captains

<u>Captain James "Bully" White</u> was in charge of the *Mermaid* in 1859 and he then commanded the *Blue Jacket* 1865-1869. The Blue Jacket was lost to fire off the Falkland Islands with a lot of the crew lost at sea. Luckily Captain White, his passengers and six crew members were picked up by a barque and survived.² He also was captain of the *Charlotte Andrews*, and then brought the *Zealandia* out to Lyttelton on her second voyage arriving 2 December 1870. Captain James White was also known as Captain "Bully" White due to his sternness towards his crew and nature of not suffering fools kindly, he was also a regimental follower of protocol and book following. He was a real hard sailor-man who delighted to carry on, and never took a sail in until he was absolutely compelled to do so. Despite this or perhaps because of this he was a well respected member of society and always mentioned with well regard on his arrival to Lyttelton. Later in the book you will discover that the *Zealandia* was to be his last vessel as tragedy struck them in 1872.

<u>Captain Henry Rose</u> commenced his career in the NZ trade by bringing out the *Mermaid*, of White Star line to Auckland in 1861. This was his second voyage as Commander. When he arrived Home the White Star Company was in difficulties and he was offered, and accepted command of the *Merope* (Shaw Savill Line), 1872. He made three voyages in this ship then joined the New Zealand Shipping Company in which he purchased an interest and brought out their first new ship *Rakaia* sailing from London in 1874 to Lyttelton. When he got back to London he took command of the *Waimate*, 1875. He

then sailed on the Waikato in 1875. While in the colony he was offered and accepted the position of Marine Superintendent for the company and the following year the directors appointed him manger of the newly opened Wellington office. He took over on August 1 1874 and year the office until he retired in 1898. He made his first voyage in the Orestes. He spent 27 years at sea and died in London in his 79th year. One of his daughters married Mr. C.V. Houghton, manager of the Auckland branch of the N.Z. Shipping Co.³

CAPTAIN H. ROSE.

<u>Captain George Sellars</u> commanded the *Bombay* 1862-1866. He commanded the *Electra* 1869-1873. Captain Sellars was in command of the *Zealandia* when she collided with the *Ellen Lamb* in 1877 mid ocean and cut her in two. He was in command of the *Bombay* to Auckland when she arrived there with all her masts gone. He commanded the *Zealandia* from 1874 - 1882. He was appointed "Ships Husband" in London in 1882. A Ship Husband is a person appointed by the ship-owner as the ships official custodian.

<u>Captain R. W. Bate</u> commanded the *Zealandia* 1891- 1901. He had previously commanded the *Langstone 1894-1895*.

<u>Captain Thomas E. Phillips</u> commanded the *Zealandia* 1884 – 1890. He had formerly commanded the *Euterpe*.⁴

Captain Curry commanded the *City of Dunedin* from 1870–1872 and the *Lady Egidia* before sailing the *Zealandia* from 1872–1873. He was a household name in the Otago region for delivering many emigrants to that area of New Zealand.[5]

Captain W. Ruth(e) commanded the *Helen Denny* for nine years, bringing many emigrants to the Hawkes Bay region. He was transferred to the *Zealandia* which he sailed to Auckland in 1883 before leaving Shaw, Savill and Albion Co. to settle in New Zealand. He lived in Napier, then Auckland and then purchased the island of Taratoroa and took up farming. He was appointed to the management of the fish market by the Auckland Harbour Board in 1889.[6] The Salvation Army bought the Ruthe family's island in the Hauraki Gulf, which is now called Rotoroa Island, in 1908 for £400.[7]

The Crew

By law all emigrants crossing the seas from England to New Zealand had to have their names and occupations written into the ship's log. These were officially recorded again at their port of arrival, however this was not always the case for the crew. Quite often sailors unofficially emigrated; they worked for their passage but remained unrecorded in the logbooks.

The standard crew for a voyage without migrants on the *Clontarf* consisted of the Captain, First Mate or Officer, Second Mate, a midshipman (apprentice officer), ship's carpenter, boatswain, 9-10 able and ordinary seamen, and the "boy" or cabin boy, used for mundane low level duties. With emigrants to accommodate, *Clontarf's* crew doubled to at least 40. Amongst the new crew were the ship's Doctor and Constable, both essential for the welfare of the passengers. For the wealthy Chief Cabin passengers there were stewards; some who were tasked to provide around the clock service for those that paid for the privilege. Other important additions to the crew were the Ship's Cook and Passenger's Cook. The main difference being that the Passenger's Cook made basic food for the masses; the Ship's Cook catered for the refined tastes of the Chief Cabin, Second Cabin and the crew. With woman and children aboard there was the need for a matron to keep the single woman apart from the single men, and also for a teacher to keep the children learning and out of the crew's way. On occasion there was a priest or minister present on the voyage.

The average crewman could earn around £7 (NZ$950) a month for the journey and were well fed with very comfortable accommodation. However the bulk of the wage was in the return voyage which could be as high as £100 each. This was paid as an incentive for loyalty and commitment to the voyage. But the hellish pace set by some captains meant that mutinies and port desertions were not uncommon.

Apprentice Williams and others making sennit mats aboard Zealandia 1869

PASSENGER LINE OF PACKETS.

SPECIAL NOTICE TO PASSENGERS.

THE Splendid Iron Clipper Ship
ZEALANDIA,
1116 Tons Register,
G. SELLARS ... ... Commander,
Will Sail for London, on or about the
5th DECEMBER.

The above ship will carry an experienced surgeon, and is provided with every accommodation for passengers.
For rate of passage money, apply to
    E. PEARCE,
    W. & G. TURNBULL & CO.,
    MURRAY, COMMON & CO.,
Or, LEVIN & CO.,
                      Agents.

Evening Post 4 December 1878

WANTED, by four Single Young Men, from England by the ship Zealandia, EMPLOYMENT of any description, either up country or in town—the latter preferred. Address J. H., office of this paper.   2599

The Star, 6 January 1871

SHIP ZEALANDIA, FROM LONDON.

GOODS CLEARED and FORWARDED, at the usual charges, by the undersigned.
           J. A. BIRD,
Licensed Custom House Agent.
Offices : Cashel street.   4832

The Star 9 December 1871

The Ship

Zealandia's Voyages from England
1869-1901

	Destination.	*Sailed.*	*Arrived.*	*Captain.*	*Days.*
1869	Lyttelton.	Aug. 18	Nov. 20	Rose	84
1870	Lyttelton.	Sept. 23	Dec. 23	White	91
1871	Lyttelton.	Sept. 8	Dec. 9	White	92
1872	Bluff and Port Chalmers.	Oct. 8	Dec. 28 Jan. 4 (1873)	Curry	88
1873	Port Chalmers.	Aug. 29	Nov. 29	Curry	92
1874	Auckland.	July 8	Oct. 15	Sellars	98
1875	Port Chalmers.	July 17	Oct. 27	Sellars	102
1876	Wellington.	June 16	Sept. 18	Sellars	94
1877	Wellington	June 4	Oct 26	Sellars	112
1878	Wellington.	May 30	Aug. 28	Sellars	90
1879	Wellington.	July 7	Oct. 19	Sellars	104
1880	Port Chalmers.	July 20	Oct. 21	Sellars	94
1881	Auckland.	June 5	Sept. 28	Sellars	115
1882	Port Chalmers.	July 9	Oct. 10	Sellars	93
1883	Auckland.	June 2	Sept. 6	Ruth(e)	96
1884	Wellington.	Apr. 16	July 18	Phillips	93
1885	Wellington.	June 16	Sept. 29	Phillips	105
1886	Lyttelton.	July 10	Oct. 16	Phillips	98
1887	Auckland.	July 24	Nov. 8	Phillips	107
1888	Auckland.	Aug. 8	Dec. 7	Phillips	120
1889	Wellington.	June 15	Sept. 15	Phillips	92
1890	Auckland.	May 31	Sept. 17	Phillips	109
1891	Lyttelton.	May 9	Aug. 10	Bate	93
1892	Port Chalmers.	Apr. 27	Aug. 2	Bate	95

1893	Wellington.	June 29	Oct. 6	Bate	99
1894	Wellington.	Sept. 4	Dec. 11	Bate	93
1895	Port Chalmers.	Aug. 17	Nov. 25	Bate	97
1897	Bluff.	May 29	Sept. 10	Bate	104
1898	Bluff.	June 22	Sept. 26	Bate	96
1899	Bluff.	June 29	Oct. 4	Bate	97
1900	Nelson.	Oct 6	Jan. 13 (1901)	Bate	98
1901	Nelson & Bluff	Sept 17	Dec. 15	Bate	97

The Zealandia at the wharves, Port Chalmers, 1116 tons. (State Library of Victoria)

The Province of Canterbury Immigration Scheme

In 1854 the provincial governments became responsible for immigration. The Province of Canterbury had the largest immigration scheme of all the provinces, bringing in almost a fifth of all immigrants between 1858 and 1870. Two thirds of all passengers arriving in Canterbury were assisted; generally, half of their fare paid by the Provincial Government.[10]

NEW ZEALAND.—The PASSENGERS' LINE.—

Ships.	Tons.	Ports.	To Sail.
City of Auckland	1,000	Auckland	Sept. 7
Caduceus	1,000	Auckland	Sept. 30
Queen Bee	1,200	Wellington	Sept. 10
England	1,200	Wellington	Sept. 30
Zealandia	1,500	Canterbury	Sept. 6
Charlotte Gladstone	1,500	Canterbury	Sept. 30
Celaeno	1,200	Canterbury	Oct. 20
Harvest Home	1,000	Canterbury	Nov. 15
City of Dunedin	1,500	Otago	Sept. 10
Warrior Queen	1,500	Otago	Sept. 30
Rapido	600	Nelson and Napier	Sept. 5
Malay	500	Wanganui	Sept. 20

The above-named ships are all first-rate passenger packets, fitted and equipped upon plans founded upon long experience.—Shaw, Savill and Co., 34, Leadenhall-street, London.

N.B. To be obtained from the above, the 12th edition of the "New Zealand Handbook," just published, post free, 1s.

30 August 1871 The Times (London)

The price for a steerage ticket was anywhere from £8 to £20, but on average most fares were around £13. In 1863 rival company Shaw, Savill & Co. secured the contract for carrying emigrants to Otago, the fares being £12 from Glasgow and £13 10s from London.[11] They had the majority of the market at this time.

Shaw, Savill & Co. had set the charges for passengers on the *Zealandia* as follows:

	1870	1871	1872	1873	1875
Single person	£14 10s	£14 15s	£13	£14	£14 10s
Couple	£29	£29 10s	£26	£28	£29
Child	£7 5s	£7 7s 6d	£6 10s	£7	£7 5s
Infant	free	free	free	free	free

There is no mention of the cost for cabin passengers on the *Zealandia* but for the *Clontarf* from 1855-57, Willis Gann were charging £60 for one person in a chief cabin measuring 6 by 7ft, or £40 each for two people. The second cabins were 6ft 9in by 7ft 6 in and for four people this cost £25 per person. Also available were second cabins for married couples measuring 3ft 6in by 7ft 8in at £25 per person.[12] It is likely the prices would have increased for cabin passengers in the 1870s and 1880s.

The average annual wage for a housemaid in 1850's-1860's was from £11-£14[13] therefore the full cost of the journey was a full years wage. The average annual wage for a farm labourer in England and Wales in 1860 was £30 2s 4p[14], so the full cost of the journey was over a third of their annual wage. We can now see that travel to New Zealand was expensive and what a struggle it was to raise even half the fare. They often had help from family and friends in the colony, and the Provincial Government would assist by paying part of the fare.

Life on Board a Clipper Ship

The food on board an immigrant ship was one of the most interesting parts of the journey for many passengers. The following chart is a Shaw, Savill & Co. Chart from 1863.

ARTICLES.		ARTICLES.	
Preserved Meats	1¼ lb.	Butter	4 oz.
Soups and Bouilli	—	Cheese	6 oz.
York Hams	—	Currants	¼ lb.
Fish	—	Raisins, Valentia	¼ lb.
Salt Beef	1 lb.	Suet	8 oz.
Pork	1 lb.	Pickles	¼ pt.
Biscuit	2 lb. 10 oz.	Mustard	¼ oz.
Flour	3½ lb.	Pepper	¼ oz.
Rice or Oatmeal	1¼ lb.	Salt	2 oz.
Barley	—	Potatoes, Fresh, or	3 lb.
Peas	½ pt.	Preserved ditto	¼ lb.
Sugar, Raw	1 lb.	Molasses, West India	¼ lb.
Lime Juice	6 oz.	Carrots	¼ lb.
Tea	2 oz.	Celery Seed	¼ oz.
Coffee, Roasted	3 oz.		

Food chart for a steerage passenger on a Shaw, Savill & Co. ship in 1863

There was different food allocated to the different classes of passengers.[12] There was usually lime juice served to keep away the scurvy. People either loved or hated the food choices. The salted beef was one example that polarized people.

Records show that there were usually, fowl in coups to produce eggs and meat, and sometimes larger animals for fresh meat. Water was stored in barrels and became stale and often grew algae or had vermin fall in and die. Sometimes there was a condensing machine on board for fresh water. Food was stored in lidded barrels but if someone left the lid off they could often become contaminated with rat and mice droppings. The bad hygiene often led to dysentery, cholera and many deaths on board. Flour often had weevils. Illness was rife on some journeys, especially when steerage passengers were confined below decks during massive storms in the Southern Ocean. The ships were cleaned with vinegar and chloride of lime to remove vomit and make things smell better, while precious water was kept for drinking.

Toileting on ships was not pleasant. Often pieces of rag, soaked in vinegar, were hung on the back of the toilet door. These were used to wipe with and were shared over and over often leading to dysentery! The sewage was often flushed into the bilge with buckets of water until emptied at port. The bilge was below steerage so the stench was not pleasant. People would be horrified these days but back then hygiene was generally not understood.[15]

Married couples' accommodation in steerage: bunks to the left and right; central table; light from the uncovered hatch. (London Illustrated News, 13 April 1844)

The sleeping arrangements were bunk beds for steerage with single women and single men having their own areas. Families often became separated as, most of the time, children over the age of 12 were transferred to the single men's or single women's quarters. Bedding was aired in fine weather but often became soaked if water was coming into the ship and this led to influenza and pneumonia outbreaks.[15]

Some ships were better managed than others. The *Zealandia* was, it seems, a well managed ship with no major outbreaks of life threatening illness reported.

On the more positive side, a ship journey such as this would have been one of life's biggest adventures for the emigrants. They would see and experience things they never dreamed of, including strange sea creatures, new constellations in the skies and a sea voyage which most would never repeat again in their lifetime, culminating in a strange new land at the final port. At night the passengers entertained each other with music, lectures of the new country and games, made new friends and contacts and looked forward to a brighter future in their new country.

A Letter Home

The following letter is an example of what immigrants would have written home to their families. This letter is from Michael Seyb(e) who travelled on the *Zealandia* in 1870. It has been translated from German to English. It is fortunate that the owner of the letter back in Germany had the foresight to publish it in 1910, in a journal. Now we have it to enjoy in the present day.[16]

Timaru, 30th January 1871

Dear Mister K. Seyb and family,

To fulfill my promise, I have the duty to take the pen in my hand and give you an insight into my life.

I will now give you a review of my journey from Germany. I departed from Kindenheim on the 12th of September; after a journey of 2 days on the Rhine and 1 day on the Nordsee I reached London, this big, dark and unhealthy city, where I never wished to live.

Bravely, I boarded the ship Zealandia on the 21st of September and on the 22nd the ship left the harbour supported by a steam boat.

After we had travelled for some days on the sea, we saw a French warship; our ship hoisted the English flag and passed the ship very close.

On the 2nd of November we passed the "sunline" [equator], and on 18th of November we reached towards the west coast of Africa. Then we came from the Atlantic Ocean into the Indian Ocean; this is the roughest sea. On 27th of November we saw Prince Edward Island; English estate. On 30th of November we saw big icebergs from the south Arctic, where once was the heat, is now the cold. From 23rd of November to 10th of December our ship travelled 5044 miles. A steam ship would never make that progress in the deep sea.

Until we reached the Cape of Good Hope we saw ships almost every day, not anymore.

On the right hand is America, on the left hand Africa. On 20th of December we saw the first ground of New-Zealand and on the 23rd we reached the harbour. The direction of the ship was south west until the equator, then it moved south until it was 52 latitudinal lines away from the equator, then south-eastern until we saw the icebergs. Then it sailed eastern until the 10th of December, north-eastern until the 18th of December, then it moved north. I have watched these directions from the sun; to convince myself I entered sometimes, as the captain and the first and second coxswain were away the compass, I had the permission from the third coxswain.
Sometimes you saw something beautiful on sea, mainly when the sun went down and the weather was fine, but sometimes also unpleasant things, the waves went over board and often the ship hang over on one side, so that you almost could touch the water with your hands.

But happily our ship reached the harbour of Lyttelton after a journey of 92 days.

Our Captain White had bad luck with his last journey to New Zealand. He had loaded cotton [flax] and it was not dried enough and inflamed and the ship "Blue Jacket" burned out. The crew were rescued by small boats. A Dutch ship found them, after they were 8 days at sea, they were half starved but the ship brought them happily at last to Melbourne in Australia.

I arrived safely in Christchurch and met all people from Kindenheim in good health conditions. I also spoke to Mister Zinckgraf. His profession is music teacher and he has a good life here, he also said that he already sent two letters to Kindenheim, but hasn't received any response. He will write to Kindenheim again and if he gets no response he will quit with writing, the same is his family.

Now I want to ask, how are you and your family doing. Hopefully in good health. The war between the Germans and French hasn't found an end yet. In 30 or 35 days we will receive a message from Germany and every 14 days from San Francisco, America and also from Suez. The latter brought a message from Germany at Christmas time to New Zealand on 25th of January.

That's very fast, although London is 15 or 16 thousand English miles away from New Zealand.

Farewell to your family and you will always live in my memories, as long as I remember and think about Germany and never forget what you have done for me, my thanks therefore.

Michael Seyb.

The Ship

The Zealandia, painting by Jill England

Map of a *Zealandia* Journey

The following map shows the 1870 journey of the *Zealandia* from London to Lyttelton. This is the typical route taken to New Zealand.

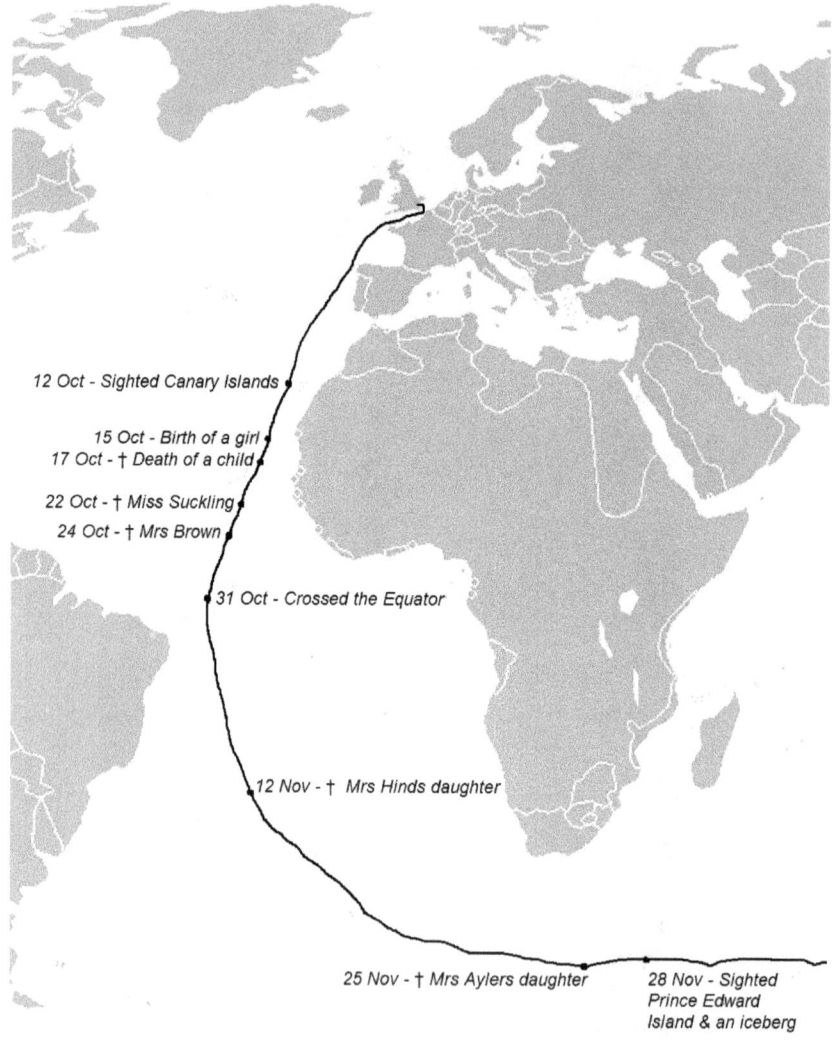

The Ship

The Demise of the *Zealandia*

In 1892 the *Zealandia* had completed a record of thirty-two round voyages to New Zealand and back to London, an amazing achievement for any ship in those days.

The *Zealandia* was sold to Russians in 1908 and was renamed *Kaleva*. The owners registered the ship in Aktiebolaget Imatra, Viborg. It was only three years later than this majestic ship was stranded on the Northumbrian coast in 1911, and her last known location was recorded in 1919 when she was being used as a barge at St John, New Brunswick, Canada. A sad ending for a once much loved and a beautifully built vessel.[1]

A stranded immigrant ship (City of Cashmere, Timaru, 1882)

Disastrous Voyages

The Death of Captain White.

Return Voyage to England - 30 souls on board. 14th April 1872.
South Pacific Ocean

Latitude 53 degrees 30 minutes South - Longitude -104 degrees West

On the 13th of April 1872 during her return voyage to England, the *Zealandia*, her Captain James White, her crew and a small handful of passengers encountered strong winds which by the 14th presented itself to be a full blown hurricane. The crew battled on relentlessly through the day as mighty winds and destructive waves hammered the ship. At 1pm the boatswain (the supervisor of the unlicensed members of the crew) was washed from the forecastle and thrown against the poop-stair opening knocking him unconscious, some thought dead. He was quickly carried to the captain quarters where he was revived.

One man down, the men returned to fight on through the day, the storm escalating with every hour. By 6pm they were tiring but it was then that the seas opened up and unleashed their fury. A wave crashed down on them so furiously that all who did not have a firm hold on anything were knocked from their feet and thrown about the ship like rag dolls. The life boats and animals that had been secured on deck, the chickens, sheep and live stock were all carried away into the water in one unforgiving onslaught. Captain White and a Second cabin passenger, Mr. C. R. Kennaway, were seen at the time to  be struggling with the ships wheel when the ferocious wave hit, both men were carried away and thrown overboard in an instant. The crew watched in horror as they disappeared into the angry waters. To make matters worse the wheel had been struck so hard it became stuck, turning the ship into the wind, tearing at the sails and throwing the ship forward, driving the front deep into the water. One crew member tried in vain to throw a life preserver over for the lost men, but it was hurtled about in the gale and disappeared in to the ocean. A short time later a returning wave was to throw Kennaway's lifeless body back onto the deck of the ship.

There was little time for the event to sink in when another violent wave hit. This time it crashed down on the boat and tore through the cabins, laying waste to the saloon where the passengers had been cowering. It tore the front off the saloon and snatched tables and chairs, even the piano overboard. The passengers scrambled out of the torrent's way with the waters chasing them, roaring into the captain and crew's quarters, filling the lower bulks with so much water that all were sure she was soon going to sink in a matter of minutes. Those on board held on for dear life and accepted the fate that was about to be decided for them. Amazingly after some time the crew managed to cut the main brace and free the stuck wheel, turning the ship about. Sadly at this time Alexander Costophine, who was hauling in the main braces, was knocked overboard, and Thomas Perrett, the second steward, was struck down and severely injured. Hours passed before the storm seemed to tire of its vengeance and slowly dissipated. By daylight the passengers and crew could not believe they had made it. In bewilderment they set about bailing out the water and repairing the ship as the chief officer Mr. King, now captain, took control and decided to head east to South America for emergency repairs at Valparaiso, Chile. *Zealandia* spent five weeks in the port there, so large was the amount of damage. Even once she was set back out to sail home to England, another leak was discovered and they were forced to return to port after only a few days at sea.

Collision with the *Ellen Lamb*

Gravesend to Wellington under Captain Sellars - 80 souls on board.
7th July 1877 – Atlantic Ocean.

Latitude 06 degrees 46 minutes north - Longitude -29 degrees 31 minutes west

After setting sail from London on 4th June 1877 *Zealandia* fell into a comfortable pace flanked by two ships, the *Niagara* and the *Ellen Lamb*. The later was a barque that had left Liverpool 37 days before-hand and was on route with a full cargo of coal to Callao, Peru. The three ships had communicated that morning and all was well as night fell.

At 10:25pm that night a passenger recalled that he was having his final pipe on the deck before turning in for the evening. It was a quiet still night, and all three ships were gliding effortlessly through the gentle waves in complete darkness as there was no moon in the sky and only starlight to guide their way.

On board the *Ellen Lamb*, which was sailing to the left of *Zealandia*, Captain James Chambers had come up on deck for his final survey of his ship before heading to his cabin. Not knowing that only a short moment beforehand the Chief Mate had already set the helm, the absentminded captain reversed the wheel and locked it hard to port and wandered off to bed, unwittingly turning the ship into the path of the unsuspecting *Zealandia*.

The first hint of trouble for *Zealandia* was when the passenger, who was smoking on deck, heard the night-watchman yell, "Light on the port bow!" The passenger and crewmen watched the green light of the *Ellen Lamb*'s starboard side close in. This indicated she was crossing *Zealandia's* path, which at that moment was illegal as *Zealandia* stood with the firm right of way.

They watched a short while longer waiting for the *Ellen Lamb* to show the port side red signal light indicating she would pass behind them, the night-watchmen cursing out loud "Show red, show red, damn you!" He then remarked to the passenger in a panic that if *Ellen Lamb* didn't slow pace soon they were going to hit.

By now the crew had heard the night-watchman's call and scampered up onto the deck, watching in horror. "Will they never give way?" a crewmen yelled, "surely they must be mad!"

When it became apparent that a collision was imminent the crew jumped to action. The Chief Mate yelled, "Back the fore-yard!" in an effort to turn the ship. But it was a fruitless effort. The crew staggered back in horror as the *Ellen Lamb*'s mast and rigging loomed out of the darkness and into full view. All on board knew that it was too late to avert the disaster.

The passenger who had been on deck fled to the lower quarters to raise the alarm, just as the terrifying call to "brace for impact" was shouted from above decks.

What followed, in the words of the passengers, was a moment of chilling silence as they awoke and fought to comprehend what was about to happen. Then a deafening earth shattering crash shook the ship to its core, the passengers thrown forward as the impact finally came.

On-board the stricken *Ellen Lamb* the crew, who had thought at first the *Zealandia*, was bearing down on them had tried to turn the ship at the last minute. The Captain and First Mate fighting over which direction the ship should have been in, while the crew were yelling at *Zealandia* to make way. When it became apparent it was too late they braced and the *Ellen Lamb* was dealt the full brunt of the large *Zealandia* hitting her midsection.

The *Zealandia* sliced right through the ship's hull. The impact tore the inner-sections, splitting the deck in two. The crew, tangled up in the ropes of the downed masts struggled for freedom, completely disoriented.

On the deck of *Zealandia* it was a "terrifying" scene of chaos. The mast and riggings collapsed, mangled and torn around the crew of the *Zealandia* as they fought to gauge what was happening. One passenger who had run up to the top to assist suddenly saw an unfamiliar face on deck, realising only later that one of the crew from the *Ellen Lamb*, had in the confusion, actually fallen onto the decks of the *Zealandia*. Such was the violence of the impact.

The *Ellen Lamb* was torn to shreds; those that had been thrown from the ship clambered up the now downed main mast of the *Zealandia* to safety or were pulled from the water by the *Zealandia*'s crew. One crewman of the *Ellen Lamb*, the cook, recounted how once on the *Zealandia* his crewmen ran to the sides to aid other crew members up from the deck of the damaged ship. The captain of the *Ellen Lamb*, who was described as an "old man" was demanding they throw down a rope cursing, "Throw me a rope, you devils!" though being unable to grab it when they did. Other crewmen yelled that the young apprentice Alfred Stevenson was tangled in the ropes and begging for help.

Zealandia's masts had been torn to shreds by the collision, and at that time it was not known what damage had been done to the front of the ship. The crew yelled, "Is she alright, will she go down?" They had little time to wonder as less than five minutes from the moment of impact someone yelled that the *Ellen Lamb* was going down.

Those on deck ran to the side and watched her sink. The cries of horror echoing about the still waters from those watching, unable to get those still left on the ship to safety

Twelve of the 16 crew escaped, but the captain of the *Ellen Lamb*, James Chambers, seaman John Jones, carpenter Robert Hudson and a young apprentice Alfred Stevenson went down with her into the dark waters. The crew of the *Zealandia* were sure that they were soon to follow her.

A man ran to the Chief Mate and yelled that there was a hole big enough to fit a horse in the port bow. All able-bodied men ran to the front and realised that the hull had not been completely breached, water only getting into the first bulk head. However the ship's mast was all but destroyed and large parts had been dragged down with the *Ellen Lamb* to her watery grave.

> **THE SHIP ZEALANDIA IN COLLISION.**
>
> **CAPTAIN OF THE ELLEN LAMB DROWNED.**
>
> The ship Zealandia, one of Messrs. Shaw, Savill's line, commanded by Captain Sellars, which left London for Wellington on the 6th June, with about 50 first and second class passengers, was in collision on the 7th July. The following particulars are from the European Mail to hand this morning:—
>
> *The Evening Post, 20 September 1877*

All souls on-board *Zealandia* came up onto the deck, some crying, others praying and thanking the Lord they were still alive. Distressed screams of children and arguing from the men who, in their confused state, sought to find someone to blame. The captain walked amongst the gathering and hushed everyone, begging for calmness. The crew put to work, calling upon all the young men of the crew to do their part and help with the pumping.

It became apparent a great while later that they were out of immediate danger, a miracle to be held considering the violence of the impact. Parts of the hole were patched with tar and scraps from the ships mast, even the scattered remains of the *Ellen Lamb* were put to use.

By morning the exhausted crew and passengers watched the sunrise with new hope. They had made it, it was all over. They turned the ship and limped her in the direction of Rio. There the mast needed to be completely replaced and the front section was painstakingly restored.

Later an inquiry would find the captain of the *Ellen Lamb* was completely at fault and *Zealandia*'s captain and crew were exonerated and revered for their bravery.

Due to the date of the accident, being the 7th day of the 7th month of the year 1877, a large number of those involved, from the *Zealandia* and the *Ellen Lamb*, tattooed themselves with the number 7777 to commemorate their brush with death.

The ship Torrens, which received similar damage as the Zealandia when she hit an iceberg.

Thirty-Two Voyages

The *Zealandia* had 32 journeys to multiple ports around New Zealand. The first journeys transported many immigrants to their exciting new home across the globe, but the final ten or so voyages were mainly cargo journeys with few or no passengers. The *Zealandia* often carried large and expensive cargos of gunpowder, discharging it before entering port. One can imagine these cargos would also be quite dangerous, with crew and passengers being ordered to keep their pipes and cigarettes away from the explosive cargo. An explosion in the open ocean would have been devastating and would probably have caused a total loss of life. Often the majestic *Zealandia* would be loaded with wool for the return trip to England, a very important trade for New Zealand, the land of sheep!

The First Three Voyages to Lyttelton 1869–1871

The first three voyages of the *Zealandia* were to the Port of Lyttelton, transporting large numbers of immigrants to the province of Canterbury.

The first New Zealand voyage left London on 18 August 1869 and arrived at port on 20 November 1869. She sailed into port at 11pm in the darkness of a spring November night with Captain Henry Rose in charge; a much respected and well known gentleman. Several cheers went up when they saw the *S.S. Gazelle* come along side and everyone seemed happy and healthy on board. It was a successful and fast voyage being only 77 days from land to land or 84 days from port to port. The trip was so good there was not much to say about it in the newspapers![17]

FOR LONDON DIRECT.

THE MAGNIFICENT CLYDE-BUILT CLIPPER SHIP ZEALANDIA,

A1 for 20 Years,

Henry Rose, Commander,

Is now loading for London, and will be despatched in February.

This fine ship was built specially for the Canterbury trade, and has every modern improvement in passenger accommodation. Bedding, linen, &c., provided for saloon passengers. The Second Cabin is a large house on deck, most comfortably fitted up. Intending passengers are invited to inspect the accommodation.

Apply to
    E. S. DALGETY & CO.,
        Lyttelton and Christchurch ;
    GEORGE GOULD,
        Christchurch ;
    MILES & CO.,
1·1   Lyttelton, Christchurch and Timaru.

SHIP ZEALANDIA, HENRY ROSE, MASTER, FROM LONDON.

ALL CLAIMS against the Inward Cargo of this Ship must be RENDERED to the undersigned on or before WEDNESDAY, the 5th JANUARY, otherwise they will not be recognised.

    MILES & CO.,
1·3   Lyttelton and Christchurch.

Advertisements for the Zealandia, 5 January 1870 Christchurch Press

The next year the *Zealandia* departed London on 23

September 1870 and arrived in the Port of Lyttelton two days before Christmas on 23 December 1870, commanded by Captain James White, who had been captain of the extreme clipper *Blue Jacket*. This passage was slightly longer than in 1869, being 87 from land to land or 90 days port to port. As the ship sailed into port the *S.S. Halcyon* declared the ship free of illness, and the 'tween decks in admirable shape. Captain White and head crew were applauded.[18]

One of the features of the trip included seeing a French war steamer; a privateer which showed its colours and saluted near Start Point on 26 September.[19] This war steamer fired at and possibly boarded another ship in the channel. The *Zealandia* luckily escaped full interrogation. The next day they saw an English Man of War (a three decker) and the Mate called out to them that all was well.[19]

On 29 September they saw a lot of porpoises swimming alongside the boat and some small birds called Mothers Carys Chickens and on 1 October they had some rain and saw lightning in the distance. One of the fowls got out of its coup and flew overboard and was, of course, drowned.

Three days later (4 October) four turtles were caught by the sailors and the second mate whilst in one of the ship boats. One of the turtles was trying to save its own life and tried to get away, pulling a sailor into the ocean.[19]

On 9 October a man's invalid daughter fell out of a chair, due to the rough sea, and broke both her thighs. The man was

FOR LONDON DIRECT.

THE FAVORITE CLYDE BUILT CLIPPER SHIP

ZEALANDIA,

Double A.1. at LLOYD'S, 1115 tons register,

JAMES WHITE, Commander,

IS NOW FAST LOADING,

And will be dispatched the end of

FEBRUARY.

This fine clipper is one of the highest classed ships afloat, and carries a duly qualified medical officer. The Saloon is lofty, well ventilated, and handsomely fitted up. There is a stewardess to attend to the lady passengers. The Second Cabin is a comfortable and well arranged house on deck.

A milch cow will be put on board.

Intending Passengers are invited to inspect the accommodation.

For freight or passage apply to

GEORGE GOULD,

MATHESON'S AGENCY,

DALGETY, NICHOLS & CO.,

Or MILES & CO.,

8701   Lyttelton and Christchurch.

The Press, 13 February 1871

extremely upset at the accident happening.[19]

They sighted the Canary Islands on 12 October. And the next day the sun was so hot in the tropics that it melted the pitch which was used to fill the joints in the planks of the deck. They saw many flying fish at this time also. A sight to behold![19]

A daughter was born to one of the passengers on 15 October.

A child (unnamed) died on 17 October. They were twelve months old and died of a bronchial complaint, the body being lowered into the deep waters at about 11pm.[19]

The *Zealandia* spoke the *Philip Nelson* on 18 October and Captain Nelson came on board the next day to have breakfast with Captain White.[19] Captain Nelson was well known to people in Canterbury.[18]

There was a tragic death on 22 October when Mr. Suckling's child died, the invalid child that broke her thigh(s). And the next day, joy, as a little girl was born.[19]

On 24 October they had vivid lightning and heavy thunder with tropical rain – very heavy rain, and the next day Mrs. Brown died, leaving three orphan children on board.[19]

They crossed the equator in longitude 29.30 West on 31 October.[18]

They had a concert on 3 November in front of the saloon with lots of singing. Even Captain White sang a "first rate song."[19]

On 5 November they sighted an albatross and there was another concert.[19]

A little girl of 7 months old, belonging to Mrs. Hinds, died on 12 November. Two days later they saw several whales. On 18 November an albatross was caught. Another wee girl belonging to Mrs. Aylers died on 25 November.[19]

On 28 November they encountered a snow storm. They saw Prince Edward Island and an iceberg of about 60 feet high. It was an old iceberg from the

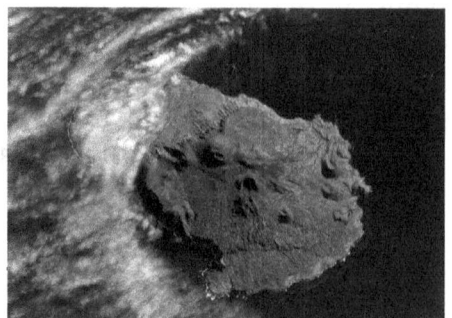

Prince Edward Island, Indian Ocean

previous year, being "ancient" in appearance,[18] which appeared on 30 November, as they were now in Sub Antarctic waters.[19]

They passed north of Kerguelen's Land but did not view it due to thick fog. On 15 December they passed Tasmania in latitude 49.19 S. and by 19 December they were south of the Snares but could not see them. [18]

Christmas Harbour, Kerguelen Island by George Cooke, 1811

On 20 December they finally saw their new homeland and passed Nugget Point at 6pm and Dunedin at 9.30pm. They sent up rockets and burnt blue lights while in sight of the town. At 11 pm they were off Cape Saunders and then the wind died down and slowed their progress.[18]

Two days later they sighted Banks Peninsula at 10 am and anchored in the harbour the next day, being 23 December. There were three births and four deaths during the voyage including two infants and two adults. They were a fine bunch of passengers having good conduct and all being in good health on arrival. The *Zealandia* proved herself to be very fast, having averaged 296 ¾ miles per day between the Cape of Good Hope and New Zealand.[18]

Captain White returned on the *Zealandia* in 1871, again with a pristinely clean ship! The journey took 89 days, port to port, departing London on 8 September and arriving on 9 December 1871. The passengers were again healthy and happy with good conduct and on board were a great group of single women with high morals. The ship had brought out a lot of animals, including some stock for Mr. J. Cracroft Wilson, of which one cow sadly died. There were also many birds which were mostly dead on arrival at Lyttelton including nightingales, larks, black caps, robins, chaffinches. Some partridges, swans, drakes and canaries were still alive.

The only casualties at sea were the animals and a lifeboat that was carried away by a heavy sea. There were two births but one was a stillborn girl.

Other highlights of the trip included crossing the Equator on 15 October at 30 degrees west. They passed Kerguelen Island and saw the mountains capped with snow, a fantastic sight for the passengers! On 7 December they sighted Cape Saunders about twenty four miles away.

They travelled at Lat 47 to 50 degrees south, once past the Cape of Good Hope, which is quite a way south compared to some journeys. This proved a fast latitude, helping the ship to travel between the meridian of Greenwich to Otago Heads in only 29 days. The *Zealandia* was again mentioned as being a superior vessel. It really was a top class ship to sail in![20]

Thirty-Two Voyages

From top clockwise: Chaffinches, English Robin, Drake, black swan, Lark, partridge, black cap, nightingale and canaries. All birds that were attempted to be transported on the Zealandia in 1871.

Two Journeys to Port Chalmers
1872–1873

The first journey left London on 8 October 1872 and arrived at Port Chalmers on 4 January 1873, via Bluff. The ship was again praised for being in "splendid order" and everything being so clean thanks to Captain Curry and the crew.

They had suffered from strong gales in the channel but managed to get to the equator on 1 November at longitude 27 degrees 15 min W.

They sighted the island of Trinidad and then on 5 December they saw the Crozet's Islands. They travelled in the Latitude of 47 degrees South and sighted Stewart Island on 26 December. The pilot boarded the *Zealandia* outside the harbour and anchored her in Port Chalmers on 28 December. The journey took 74 days from pilot to pilot. Most of the 392 passengers were landed at Bluff on 28 December 1872 with only 84 being landed at Port Chalmers, including 23 single females.

It was noted that the compartments were "beautifully fitted" especially in the single females area which had "fine airy accommodation in the after part of the poop, which was 75 feet in length, forming an ample promenade."

The *Zealandia*'s second trip to Port Chalmers departed London on 29 August and arrived on 29 November 1873, again with Captain Curry at the helm. The second journey was similar to the first in that everyone was healthy and happy and the "all well" flag was flown from the mizzen mast when she appeared at the Heads.[5]

Family and friends flocked on board to see their relations and friends, thinking that the passengers were not to be unloaded just yet. However they were wrong and the passengers were taken by the steamer *Golden Age* quickly to Dunedin and all were there only four hours after the ship's arrival. There were many "hurrahs" heard coming from the passengers on arrival, just relieved to be on land after their journey. The single men and women had excellent accommodation but the married couples and families had been herded into open berths and it was hoped that a better arrangement could be made for the next journey where there was a bit more privacy. The single women's area was noted as being so big it had been used for an "entertainment" given to the officers only a few days before anchoring in Port Chalmers.

There had been three deaths on board; a low number.

Deaths

26 September – Mary Elizabeth Hillion of disease of the brain (child)

9 October – Jane Elizabeth Stokes of diarrheoa (child)

27 October – William Knight, the ship's butcher died of a liver complaint.

Two people were injured on the voyage:

17 November a "pretty boy" named Baxter, aged 7 years, fell down the companion ladder breaking his right thigh. A similar accident happened to a female saloon passenger who fell down the companion ladder and broke her arm.

They crossed the line on 2 October at longitude 22 20 West and the meridian of the Cape of Good Hope was passed on 29 October. The saw the light of Cape Leeuwin and then a few days later, sighted Stewart Island on 28 November at 4 am.[21]

Auckland 1874

The *Zealandia*'s next trip was to Auckland in 1874 with a new master, Captain Sellars, making the journey in 90 days land to land or 96 days from Gravesend. They departed on 8 July 1874 from London. She arrived at port at half past five on 15 October 1874, with 219 immigrants and a large number of saloon and second class passengers.

The passage was longer than expected due to contrary winds at the beginning of the voyage. There were four births and two deaths during the voyage but everything on board was ship shape, as per previous voyages.

Births
15 July – Mrs. Sefton, of a girl
25 August – Mrs. Grove, of a boy
8 October – Mrs. Wright, of a girl
10 October – Mrs. Morgan, of a girl

Deaths
23 September – Mary Watson, aged 13 months of diarrhoea
6 October – Sarah Mitchell, aged 41 years, of chronic bronchitis and diarrhoea.[22]

Port Chalmers 1875

Sellars was still commanding for the next 8 voyages. His second voyage in the *Zealandia* was to Port Chalmers departing London on 17 July 1875 and arriving on 27 October of that year.

Mrs. Christapella Rogerson was a second cabin passenger who was appointed as Matron, with a sub-matron named Annie Mitchell. James Ring or King aged 21 was taken out of the ship at Gravesend by a Sheriff's Officer and Mrs. Buckingham and his supposed wife were also landed there. Mrs. Buckingham was found to be married to a different man and their plan of escape was foiled by the authorities!

The single male immigrants were exercised in boat and fire drills on the voyage whilst the single women were well guarded and supervised as per regulations. There was a school conducted by a passenger named Mr. Frederick Horne.

The doctor started the *Zealandia Gazette* to ease the monotony of the voyage. It was a weekly publication of which three copies were written, none of which are known to still exist. One was given to the after part of the ship, one for the married people and one for the single men and crew. They had private theatricals and the doctor delivered temperance speeches to the passengers, converting a few passengers by doing so. The immigrants were extremely happy with the treatment and attention of the crew and presented the doctor with three testimonials.

Again the single women had the best part of the ship with the families still needing a little more privacy, according to the reporters. The reporters didn't like the bunks which were arranged "London fashion, in blocks, with side alleys."

This voyage had a much more liberal dietary scale than on previous voyages due to new rules and regulations. There was not one case of punishment of the passengers during the voyage and no sickness.

There was one death though, of Daniel Gabbins, aged 32, on 2 August from inflammation of the brain and only one birth, a daughter to Mrs. Harvey who was confined on 16 September.

Highlights of the journey included crossing the Equator on 25 August in Longitude 27 West and rounding the Cape on 22 September. They sighted the high mountainous peak of Tristan d'Acunha on 12 September.

From the Cape to Tasmania the ship was caught in very unsettled weather and winds. On 25 September the ship passed an iceberg in lat. 43 South, Long. 32.6 E. It was about 300 feet long and 100 feet high and "pretty well water-worn."

Tristan D'Acunha

The sight however would have been amazing. It was 24 October before they sighted the Snares and with bad winds they crept slowly along the coast to Port Chalmers.

Wellington 1876–1879

The *Zealandia* had four trips in a row to Wellington with

Captain Sellars at the helm.

The ship left London on 16 June 1876 on its first Wellington voyage. A highlight of the 1876 trip included crossing the line on 19 July in 25.30 W. They had a good run from the Cape to Tasmania in the Roaring Forties but had trouble getting into the harbour at Wellington, finally anchoring on 18 September 1876. The fastest run they had in a day was 291 knots and the smallest was 16 knots. There were very few passengers on board. Before leaving for England she was loaded with wool, being the first wool ship of the season.

The journey in 1877 is outlined in "Disastrous Voyages." It was truly a terrible time for the passengers and the ship was lucky to survive.

In 1878 the *Zealandia* brought no government immigrants and just 46 paying passengers. She left at the same time as the *Halcione* for Auckland on 30 May 1878, but parted with her after being eight days in her company. There was only one bad gale experienced which carried away the poop skylight. They arrived into Wellington on 28 August 1878.

Another trip to Wellington in 1879 saw the ship again filled with government immigrants, all 346 of them! Plus there were two paying saloon passengers. They departed London on 7 July 1879. There were two cases of chicken pox on arrival on 19 October, so the ship had to have a cleaning and fumigation before it could pratique (gain a license to enter the harbour after being assessed for illness).

They crossed the Equator on 19 August at Longitude 23 degree W. The Cape of Good Hope was passed on 15 September and Cape Farewell was sighted on 17 October at 4pm.

Port Chalmers 1880

The 1880 voyage to Port Chalmers again had Captain Sellars at the helm, being now very experienced at sailing the ship *Zealandia*. The journey took 86 days from land to land or 94 days from the London Docks on 20 July 1880 to anchorage at Port Chalmers on 21 October. The vessel was in first rate condition, as it usually was, bringing 35 passengers.

They experienced light westerly winds and thick foggy weather in the English Channel. It wasn't much better in the Bay of Biscay with adverse westerly winds. They met S. W. monsoons at latitude 15.11 N, longitude 26.10 W. which included heavy rain and squally weather. The Cape of Good Hope was rounded on 18 September at latitude 40 S. There were gales at times with very high seas breaking on board and causing the ship to labour heavily. The ship took on quite a lot of water during this time. The meridian of Cape Leeuwin was crossed in latitude 46.30 S. The Snares were sighted on 19 October and *Zealandia* came up the coast until the pilot came on board on 21 October to take her into Port Chalmers. It was noted that no ice or wreckage was spotted during the passage!

THE NEW ZEALANDIA AT PORT CHALMERS.

Auckland 1881

Captain Sellars again commanding the *Zealandia*, departed London on 5 June 1881 and arrived at Auckland on 28 September 1881. He anchored off the end of the Queen-street Wharf. They sighted Trinidad on 3 August and on 6 September there was a heavy northerly gale and the ship took on a lot of water. The starboard quarter boat and port skid boat were both damaged. The starboard and port davits were also broken. A lot of water went down below and would have needed to be pumped out. They made the Three Kings Islands on 25 September and then travelled down to the port of Auckland. There were no deaths or illness on board and one birth to a Mrs. Verrier who was confined with a female child and both were doing well. Apart from meeting with two scary and dangerous gales it was a pleasant voyage with a lot of fine weather. The greatest days travel was 316 miles or knots and the least, 47 miles!

Three Kings Islands by Peter Southwood. Creative Commons Attribution License 3.0

Henry Brett's book *White Wings* has a testimonial from a Mrs. F. A. Davies (nee Goodwyn) who was on the 1881 voyage. It was similar to the journey the year after which was horrifically scary for the passengers. "We had a similar experience [to 1882], the captain remarking to me that he had never passed through a more anxious time. We had a cargo of gunpowder and a large number of third-class passengers, many of whom, I remember, as soon as the storm abated, were carried from their (all but) living tomb and laid upon the poop deck in a state of exhaustion."

Port Chalmers 1882

Sellars last journey in the *Zealandia* was to Port Chalmers with some cabin passengers. They had an eventful voyage with much bad weather. Captain Sellars described it as the worst he had ever met during 30 years in the Southern Ocean. There were marks on the ship from the furious gales. The passenger's compartment was completely flooded out and they had a miserable journey. Several seamen lost the whole of their belongings, their chests having been washed overboard. There were only 22 passengers with no government immigrants. She carried much cargo including seven tons of explosive powder, stowed in a properly constructed magazine. She had to discharge it before going to the wharf.

The steward was commended for the very tidy

Trinadad and Martinique at the top of Venezuela

appearance of the saloon seeing it had been flooded and also used by the second class passengers. They left Gravesend on 9 July and arrived at Port Chalmers on 10 October 1882. From anchor to anchor the passage was 93 days long; quite long for the *Zealandia*. She had a long passage through the Channel due to bad weather clearing it on 16 July. She rounded the Cape of Good Hope on 6 September in latitude 40.28 S.[23]

The story from the journey in 1882 was very dramatic as was outlined in the newspapers. It was described as a tempestuous voyage.

"The *Zealandia* was sailing well until the ship reached latitude 42.1 S., longitude 65.19 E., when she encountered a cyclone of hurricane violence, during which both lower topsails were blown away, and the ship ran under bare poles, while tremendous seas broke on board, and carried away the forecastle and head rails, pig pens, front of the deckhouse, and washed the contents of the galley entirely out. The doors of the deckhouse were burst in, the water tanks were stove in, and the sheep pens smashed in two; while a considerable portion of the top-gallant bulwarks and the rail were carried away. During the gale the barometer fell to 28.70. Captain Sellars stated that the ship behaved splendidly throughout, but owing to the sea being so high and cross, she had very little fair play. The weather calmed down on about 18 September, and all hands were employed in repairing damages and bending fresh sails. She then experienced fresh to light breezes, accompanied by a very heavy S.W. swell, and was constantly shipping great quantities of water. On September 28, in latitude 45.2 S., longitude 120.1 E., the barometer began to fall very rapidly, and the wind came out W.N.W., increasing to a heavy gale. The vessel was put under her two lower topsails and run before it. "The gale increased to frightful violence on September 30, attended by a high cross sea, which broke on board, filled the main deck and washed away everything movable, so that by noon nothing was left. You can imagine the distress of the passengers. Several heavy following seas were then encountered, which carried away the poop stairs and wing closets, and flooded the saloon—the water finding its way to the lazaret and doing considerable damage. At about 2 p.m. two tremendous seas came on board, washing away the bridge and boat skids and smashing one of the boats, bursting in the starboard door of the saloon, in which the third-class passengers were berthed, and driving the occupants completely out of their compartment into the body of the saloon. Another terrific sea then pooped her, breaking the skylights and forcing its way into the saloon, creating the greatest fear amongst the passengers, who were in a miserable plight; while the front of the forecastle was completely stove in and the seamen's chests washed overboard. Indeed, Captain Sellars stated that during the continuance of the September moon the weather was decidedly the worst, and the two gales the heaviest in all his thirty year's experience in the Southern Seas, and only to be compared with that which at times prevailed in the Bay of Bengal. The barometer, during the gale of September 30th, fell to 27.80, the sympesometer to 27.90. After passing Tasmania on 3rd October the wind freshened to another strong gale on the 5th, compelling the ship to heave to under her main topsail. The wind suddenly fell calm, and later light favourable winds enabled her to reach port on the 10th October."

"The *Zealandia* made her easting between the parallels of 42 and 43 south latitude. Notwithstanding the buffeting the ship received the passage was completed in 93 days, or 84 land to land."

Auckland 1883

Did the journey in 1882 force Captain Sellers into retirement? We are not sure, but in any case, Captain Ruthe (sometimes spelt Ruth) took over from Captain Sellars and brought the *Zealandia* into Auckland the next year, on 6 September 1883. The ship had departed London on 2 June 1883 and had a good run out of the Channel and then some contrary winds near the Madeiras which eased on 11 June. The Equator was crossed 36 days after departure in longitude 28. They ran at 45 degrees along the "easting." They made the Three Kings by 3 September, before arriving at Auckland. The ship had a cargo of 28,500 pounds including ten tons of explosive powder which had to be discharged before entering the harbour.[24]

Captain Ruthe told a story of this journey out. "The smartest thing I ever did," said Captain Ruth... "was when going into Auckland as captain of the *Zealandia*. I had received a complaint from a passenger in the second-class that he could not sleep, and I went down to inquire into it. He said to me, 'How would you like to be sleeping in your bunk and have a fellow spitting in your eye?' I said I wouldn't like it, and I shifted him away from a sick man whom I had some difficulty in getting past the health officer. Old Dr. Philson came aboard, and I lined the passengers up in two rows—45 on one side and 46 on the other - my sick man on the end. Dr. Philson came and had a look at the passengers of the 45 row, and passed them all. Just as he got to the end of the row I shifted the sick man to the head of the other line, and I saved my company £500."[25]

Wellington 1884–1885

Captain Phillips took over the *Zealandia* and sailed into Wellington Harbour, with some cabin passengers, on 18 July 1884, departing London on 16 April 1884. A second class passenger named Hannah had problems with the rats on board. On Friday 2 May she wrote: "... at about 4.30 I heard a gentle rustling overhead. Presently I saw the cause of it! A monster rat jumped off Ruth's bunk. I was rather scared but felt determined to bear with his company if possible without waking anyone else, and I was rewarded by seeing him walk away without nibbling anything! But not until he had made a general survey of my bunk. He came on at my feet. I could feel his little scratching nails on my bare feet, and feared every moment that he would bite, but he walked in an orderly fashion up one side of me, looking about him. On crossing my pillow he was hindered by an entanglement in my hair, at which I felt it almost impossible to keep from screaming loudly. But to my great relief he soon released himself and walked in just such an orderly fashion down the other side of me and out at a hole at the foot which he had previously made. It was a struggle for me to keep quiet. The perspiration was streaming off me like rain, but I was thankful I had the courage to keep quiet ... sleep is precious these days with heat and rats combined."

Two months later Hannah's cabin was eight inches deep in

water and she was having trouble sleeping. She wrote about the pesky rats again:

". . . Aroused at 7.30 after another very stormy night, and the rats were so troublesome. They were quarrelling and splashing about in the water making a dreadful noise all night . . . our jackets are hung on the saloon wall, they get in the pockets of them and nibble our handkerchiefs . . . They run up and down our dresses which are hanging on the wall, and over the top of the partition."

In 1885 Captain Phillips sailed to Wellington again on 29 September, a journey of 106 days from London departing 16 June 1885. He had on board a few cabin passengers and only 12 in steerage.

Lyttelton 1886

In 1886 they made an uneventful passage of 98 days with 25[26] or 35 passengers.[27] They left London on 10 July and arrived in Lyttelton on 16 October. It was Captain Phillips first trip to Lyttelton on the *Zealandia*, but he was remembered as sailing the *Euterpe* into Lyttelton a few years earlier.

Auckland 1887–1888

In 1887 they travelled to Auckland arriving 8 November 1887. The ship left London on 24 July. The equator was crossed on 1 September and the Cape rounded on 28 September. On 7 October they experienced a very heavy gale which lasted over 24 hours. The meridian of the Leeuwin was passed on 19 October and the south end of Tasmania on 26 October. They sighted the Three Kings and were then outside Auckland Harbour arriving on 8 November. The Cook died on board of general debility on 28 August. They anchored in the harbour on 8 November 1887.[4]

In 1888 it was a lengthy journey for this magnificent ship with people waiting anxiously in the Port of Auckland for its arrival. The total journey was 118 days leaving London on 8 August and arriving in Auckland on 7 December 1888. They never got the N.E. trades and the winds were very light in the first part of the journey. It took them 47 days to travel from London to the Equator. They passed many vessels, some of them extremely close. Mr. J. Gunning started up a small publication called *The Zealandia Star* which everyone contributed to.

Highlights of the journey included crossing the line on 24 September at 24 degrees West and sailing between Trinidad and Martin Islands (Martinique) on 1 October. They crossed the meridian of Greenwich on 16 October and rounded the Cape of Good Hope on 22 October at 43 degrees S. They passed the islands of St. Paul and Amsterdam on 5 November and nine days later they crossed the meridian of Cape Leeuwin. They passed the southern point of Tasmania on 22 November and sighted the Three Kings on the morning of 3 December.

Trinadad and Martinique at the top of Venezuela

Thankfully everyone on board arrived safe and healthy, apart from one passenger, a Mr. Francis J. Gardner, dying of consumption on 24 October. This apparently cast a veil of gloom over the other passengers. They delivered a load of explosives to the powder ground.[28]

Wellington 1889

In 1889 the *Zealandia* had a stormy passage to Wellington arriving 15 September. They left London on 15 June and passed the meridian of the Cape on 10 August and Tasmania on the 6 September. The terrible rough weather carried away one of the *Zealandia's* boats with the other being damaged by the heavy sea. There were only three cabin passengers on board.[29]

Auckland 1890

The *Zealandia* came back to Auckland, again with Captain Thomas E. Phillips in command. They had another load of gunpowder to deliver to the port of Auckland.

The voyage took 109 days, departing London on 31 May and arriving in Auckland on 17 September. The journey was largely uneventful. There were only two passengers on board, the daughters of Captain Phillips.

They left London on 31 May, had moderate weather down the Channel and cleared the Lizard on 7 June. The Equator was crossed on 4 July at 23 degrees W. The meridian of Greenwich was crossed on 30 July and the Cape of Good Hope four days later. They passed Tasmania on 3 September and then the Three Kings were reached at 9.30 am on 16 September.   The ship was berthed at Queen-street Wharf on 17 September.[30]

Lyttelton 1891

Captain Phillips was replaced on the 1891 journey, by Captain Bate who sailed the *Zealandia* on her last six journeys to New Zealand.

The journey in 1891 was most "uneventful" and took 93 days which was an average run, protracted slightly by the light winds. They departed on 9 May from London arriving at Lyttelton on 10 August. They didn't see a single gale, even in the Southern Ocean which was very unusual. Many ships were spoken on the line. No passengers are mentioned in newspaper accounts.[31]

Port Lyttelton, 1863 (Illustrated London News, 17 Oct 1863)

The Explosive Cargo Years 1892–1901

The *Zealandia* had already transported a lot of explosive material to New Zealand on previous voyages and this continued over the next 10 years. The *Zealandia* brought fewer passengers to the colony now and was concentrating on cargo.

The ship made a trip to Port Chalmers in 1892 departing Glasgow on 27 April and arriving in Port Chalmers on 2 August, a journey of 95 days. No passengers were mentioned. She was loaded with 560 packages of dynamite and 17 cases of detonators which were stowed away in a properly constructed magazine. The highly explosive cargo was discharged into the powder schooner *Ark*. About 1350 tons of cargo was for Dunedin and about 200 tons for Wellington. The *Zealandia* hit some very bad weather while "running down her easting," in the roaring forties. About 20 feet of gallant bulwarks and about 40ft of washboards around the poop were carried away into the mountainous seas. There was also continuous lightning right across the Southern Ocean. One of the seamen, named Pollock, died on the voyage and was buried on 22 May in lat. 12.30 N., long 25 W.[32]

In 1893 the *Zealandia* left from Liverpool on 29 June, sighted Madeira on 13 July and crossed the Equator on 3 August. They rounded the Cape of Good Hope on 29 August and arrived in Wellington on 6 October. The voyage was uneventful and the weather moderate. She discharged 20 tons of gunpowder before berthing at Queen's Wharf, Auckland, to discharge the rest of the cargo.[33]

The next year in 1894 the ship left from Liverpool again, on 4 September and arrived in Wellington Harbour on 11 December. The only interesting feature of the voyage was that in the latitude of 28 N a seaman named Fay fell overboard while working on the mizzen rigging. The ship was running before a seven-knot breeze. A boat was lowered straight away and the chief officer Mr. Cousins picked up Fay in less than 20 minutes from when he fell. Fay was in fine health after his little adventure.[34]

In 1895 the *Zealandia* sailed from Glasgow on 17 August and arrived at Port Chalmers on 25 November, having a rather long journey of 98 days from anchor to anchor. They met calms and very light winds from the Channel until they crossed the equator (42 days out). After that however they made good progress with only 32 days from the Cape to her anchorage. Two banded pigeons were caught after flying on board and had numbers on their legs which were quoted in the newspaper. She was "in that usual excellent order which has always characterized her." She had 800 tons of cargo for Dunedin and dynamite for Wellington.[35]

It was 1897 before the *Zealandia* returned. She sailed from London on 29 May and arrived at Bluff on 10 September of that year.[36] The *Zealandia* had another rough experience on this journey to Bluff on 8 August. Captain Bate stated that while the ship was hove-to during a fierce gale the fore tower topsail was blown away, foretopmast staysail split, and the mizzen storm staysail split. The ship was stripped to bare poles and thrown on her beam ends. This was a terrible thing to happen and could have resulted in a total loss of the ship.[37]

In 1898 she sailed again from London departing 22 June and experienced fine weather almost throughout the voyage arriving in Bluff on 26 September 1898.[38]

Yet another cargo journey took place in 1899 to Bluff with it hardly getting a mention in the newspapers.

Because the *Zealandia* had never sailed into Nelson before, its trip in 1900 had a huge newspaper summary. They left London on 6 October 1900 and arrived on 13 January 1901. Highlights of this journey were, sighting Cape de Verde Islands on 28 October, crossing the Equator at longitude 25 degrees W on 11 November and a large storm that lasted 12 hours. The storm caused very high seas. They also saw a lot of lightning on entering Cook Strait.[39]

The *Zealandia* made its last cargo trip to Nelson in 1901 departing London on 17 September and arriving on 15 December. Another large summary was printed in the papers. They found a stowaway on board and because the weather was calm and they were off Plymouth, they got a boat and put him on board a trawler to be landed back on shore. They passed Madeira, Salvages and Teneriffe and the town of Santa Cruz of which they saw lights at 8am on 23 September. They sailed for five days in the company of the ship *Aristidis* which was heading from London to Australia. They had moderate winds and fine weather prevailing throughout the voyage. Mr. Bate was in command with 1st Officer Beaumont, 2nd Officer Mr. Atherton and 3rd Officer, Mr. Barrow.[40]

The *Zealandia* sailed for the Bluff on 13 January 1902.[41] It then sailed from the Bluff to London on 27 February 1902 with 6068 bales of wool.[42]

The *Zealandia* was never seen on New Zealand shores again, but it remained in the memories of its passengers all their lives. It was *their* ship and had transported them to *their* new country on the other side of the world. After the trials and tribulations of a three month ocean journey, it was something they would never ever forget.

Passenger Biographies

Abraham, Mr. and Mrs. E. S., travelled to New Zealand in the *Zealandia* arriving in October 1874. Mr. Abraham was born in 1851 in England and was the son of Canon Abraham and the nephew of Bishop Abraham. Mr. E. S. Abraham took up farming at Pukekohe with his brother and then joined the Bank of New Zealand, eventually becoming manager at Bulls. He bought the firm Messrs. Stevens and Gorton in 1884 and settled in Palmerston North. He retired in 1923 and had his Golden wedding in 1930. They had a family to two sons and five daughters, and in 1930 had 21 grandchildren.

Bale, Mr. A., was a butcher in Featherston. He left Ilfracombe, Devonshire on the *Zealandia* in 1879 and travelled to Wellington. He started his business in Featherston in 1884. He also had a freehold farm of sixty acres on the town boundary. He grew sheep and cattle for his business and did his own slaughtering, which meant quality meat for his customers. He had a sausage machine driven by horsepower!

Barlow, Edwin, was a general merchant in Dee Street, Invercargill. He started the business in 1897 after arriving on the *Zealandia* to Bluff in 1872 and working for Mr. D. Roche for several years. He married in 1871 to a daughter of Mr. Charles Whellar of London and they had seven sons and six daughters.

Mr E. Barlow

Battersby, Edmund, was a resident of Petone who came to Wellington in the *Zealandia* in 1874, his fiancé following him four years later. They married on her arrival. Edmund had studied art at the Royal Academy, London. On arrival in New Zealand he founded a painting and decorating business. He died in 1934, aged 80 in Petone and was survived by a widow and two sons and three daughters.

Birch, Mr., Joseph, came to New Zealand in the *Zealandia* in about 1871. He lived for many years in Hikurangi where he mainly worked at the Hikurangi Coal Company and the Northern Coal Company. He never married. He took one trip home to see family and friends in Middlesex and Hertfordshire. He died in 1917.

Boyce, Charles, was born in Faversham Kent and came to New Zealand in the *Zealandia* in about 1873. He lived for a short time in Cambridge before moving to Napier where he married Sarah Jane Beaumont. Two years later he went back to Cambridge and never moved. He bought Holloway's General Store and ran it his whole life. He was an original member of Cambridge Town Borough Council and an early member of the Masonic Lodge Alpha and founder of the Cambridge Band and secretary and treasurer of the Anglican Church. He was a forceful character. He was often called the "Father of Cambridge." When he died of a fall at his home in 1937, aged 86 years, he had ten children still surviving (of 11) as well as 23 grandchildren and two great grandchildren.

Breen, James, was a councillor in the Waimate County Council of which he was elected to in 1902. He was born near Lake Killarney in Ireland in 1849 and came to Port Chalmers in the *Zealandia* in 1874. He spent many years doing horticultural work and road contracting and in 1883 he settled on a farm at Island Stream near Maheno where he lived for 16 years. In 1899 he settled on the Waikakahi estate. He was also director of the North Otago Dairy Factory. He married a daughter of Mr. D. Slattery of County Kerry, Ireland in 1883 and they had three sons and two daughters.

Brosnahan, Mrs. Catherine, came to Lyttelton on the *Zealandia* in 1871. She left three daughters and four sons to mourn her loss when she died in Kerrytown in 1916. She also left 80 grandchildren and 70 great grandchildren!

Buchan, Alexander, was a Railway Storeman at the Palmerston North Railway Station. He was born in 1853 in Aberdeen and came to Wellington on the *Zealandia* in 1879. He joined the Railway as a porter in Wanganui and was promoted to his position in 1886. He loved outdoor games with the Caledonian Society. In 1878 he married a daughter of Mr. Robert Johnson of Tynemouth and they had one daughter.

Caldwell, Mr. Johnston, was born in Ireland and enlisted in the 7th Light Dragoons in 1855, and served with them in India. He was transferred to the orb Lancers in India and eventually got a pension. He then travelled in 1871 on the *Zealandia* for Wellington. He took up bush falling and gumdigging until he came to the Veterans' Home in Auckland where he died in 1918.

Clark, Edwin, was a Shoeing and General Blacksmith in Waverley. He was born in Stroud, Gloucestershire, England and came to Auckland in the *Zealandia* in 1871. He did apprentice work before starting up his own business. He established his business in 1881 in Waverley. He had a house and a fine large grass paddock for which to run his cow on.

Clark, Mr. S. H., was born in Stroud, Gloucestershire and came to New Zealand on the ship *Zealandia* in 1874. He then went to California and after returning worked as a builder until he retired. He died at Herme Bay, Auckland aged 74 and was survived by four brothers.

Cluett, Mr. G. E., was born in Portsmouth, England and in 1870 entered the service of the mercantile marine. He worked for seven years for the Shaw, Savill and Albion line and became second mate on the *Zealandia*. He eventually settled in New Zealand where he had different occupations. He moved to Stratford in 1890 and took over the Commercial Hotel, then the Ellerslie Hotel, near Auckland. He then worked as a sharebroker. He eventually returned to Stratford and took over the Stratford Hotel until he finally settled at Toko.

Diver, Richard and Catherine (Nee Hegarty). Richard Diver, born in Letterkenny, Ireland in 1854 sailed on *Zealandia* in 1875 as a single-man labourer. On that same voyage was his future wife, Catherine Hegarty, who was travelling as a maid-servant to the steerage family McElhinny. Catherine, also from Letterkenny was born in 1850 and it can be assumed that both her and Richard either were travelling separately "together" or at least knew of each other's existence before boarding *Zealandia* in 1875. They were married three years later and settled in Oamaru where they had seven children. Richard spent most of his life employed as a labourer and dockworker, helping passengers ashore before the wharf was built. Sadly in 1908 Richard went to visit a friend and was thought to have slipped down a ridge into the ocean, the proof being that some weeks later his boot washed ashore with his right foot still in it. The widowed Catherine carried on with the children, and later her grandchildren, before passing away in 1923.[41,42]

Mrs Catherine Diver

Evans, Richard, was born in Montgomeryshire, Wales, England, and educated by his father, who was a bailiff of Lord Sudley, and came of an old Welsh family. He served an apprenticeship of four years to a flour miller and worked for a draper before coming to Lyttelton on the *Zealandia* in 1871. He worked for Mr. Isaac Wilson of Kaiapoi at flax dressing. He then became a carrier between Christchurch, Kaiapoi, Rangiora and Oxford. He bought a farm and became a flour miller and produce merchant. He was chairman of the

Eyreton Road Board and Waimakariri Harbour Board and Director of the Kaiapoi Building Society. He was also a member of the Temperance Lodge. He married Fanny Blackwell in 1875 and they had six children.

Garrett, William John, was a butcher in Wellington. He was born in London in 1851 and educated at the City of London School. He arrived in the *Zealandia* in 1874. He conducted his butchers business from 1881 several years after arriving. He was materially assisted in the business by his brother.

Gillingham, George, was born in Dorsetshire, England, in 1843, and came to New Zealand in 1870, in the ship *Zealandia*. He immediately settled on the West Coast, where he engaged in mining with his uncle (Mr. Lucas) for over a year, and eventually became storeman for Mr. Coates, the well-known Greymouth merchant, and afterwards with Mr. Dickie at Cobden. On the death of Mr. Dickie, in 1882, Mr. Gillingham commenced business on his own account.

Grant, George, was born in Banffshire, Scotland in 1857 and travelled to Wellington in the *Zealandia* in 1876. He studied at Otago University. In 1885 he took up teaching and eventually became headmaster of College Street School, Palmerston North. He was also a lay preacher at the Presbyterian Church and was a believer in temperance. In 1884 he married a daughter of Mr. A. Duthie, one of the pioneer settlers of Tokomariro (Milton), Otago.

Mr G. Grant

Griebel, Peter and Marie, were siblings from Kindenheim, Germany. They travelled to New Zealand in 1870 on the *Zealandia*. Marie married Jakob Ellenberger in Christchurch in 1874 and they had nine children. Peter married Emilie Bratz and they had many children also.

Both families lived and farmed in the Tuahiwi and Ohoka areas. Jakob and Marie eventually moved to Kaiapoi in later years.

Jakob and Marie Ellenberger nee Griebel

Hacon, Dr Walter Edmund, studied medicine at Guy's Hospital, London. He gained the L.R.C.P. and M.R.C.S. diplomas in 1872, and became a licentiate of the Society of Apothecaries in the following year. He was Honorary Associate of the Order of St. John of Jerusalem, and was resident accoucheur at Queen's Hospital, Birmingham, and assistant medical officer at the Central London Sick Asylum, Highgate; for three years he was resident surgeon at the Bedford General Infirmary and Fever Hospital, and subsequently assistant medical officer at York County Lunatic Asylum.

Dr. Hacon came to Wellington, New Zealand, in 1879, by the ship *Zealandia*, as surgeon-superintendent, and was appointed the first medical superintendent at Sunnyside Asylum. He occupied that position for seven years, and then he established a practice in Christchurch.

Dr. Hacon was a frequent contributor to medical literature. Dr. Hacon died on the 20th of September, 1898, from apoplexy.

Hardwick, John, was born in 1829 in Buckinghamshire, England where he learnt farming. He arrived at Lyttelton in 1870 on the *Zealandia* and starting farming near Christchurch. In 1874 he moved to Ashburton where he farmed until 1881. He then took up land in the Aparima district and farmed there until he was 70. He married Miss Foshel, of Huntingdonshire, England and they had four sons and four daughters.

Mr J. Hardwick

Hill, Mr., was born at Ludlow, Shropshire and came to Wellington in 1878 on the *Zealandia*. He was educated at Bitterley Grammar School and became a teacher at the Public School, Leominster, but he was subsequently at the training college for teachers at Bangor, North Wales. The first school held by Mr. Hill in the Colony was at Wainui-o-mata. He was then at Taonui, Normanby, Crofton, Okoia, and Waverley. In the latter town he remained as headmaster for five-and-a-half years. Mr. Hill was in charge of Feilding School from 1880. He was into chess and cricket and had a farm near Stratford consisting of 1000 acres, of which about a third was cleared, and which had enough pasture for 700 sheep.

Jarvis, Charles Bridge, was born in London in 1844 and travelled to Lyttelton on the *Zealandia* in 1871. He settled in the Kaituna Valley with his brother and died in 1914 leaving a family of four daughters and three sons.

Kennerley, Harry Bennett, was a Coach Proprietor, Livery and Bait Stablekeeper in Wellington. Mr. Kennerley was born in Cheshire, England, and came to New Zealand on the ship *Zealandia*, in 1878. Mr. Kennerley had some fine coaches and beautiful horses for his business which were ready to supply transport for picnics, wedding and other functions.

Knox, Mr. Henry, was born in Kent, England and came to New Zealand in 1871 on the *Zealandia*. He worked for three years at a confectionery works in Dunedin and was then appointed manager of Otaki Cordial Factory on establishment in 1893.

Logan, Robert, was a Senior, Designer and Builder of Yachts, Steamboats, Sailing Vessels, in Auckland. Mr. Logan was named the Fyfe of Australasia, as, like his prototype in Scotland, he was unrivalled as a designer of champion yachts and coastal steamers. He was born in Dumbarton, Scotland, in 1837, and was educated in Glasgow, where he also learned his trade with a well known firm of shipwrights. In 1874 he migrated to Auckland by the ship *Zealandia*, and worked as a journeyman until 1879, when he began to build and design yachts, at the North Shore. Since then and up to the present time he has designed and built the following coastal steamers: — The S.S. "Neptune," S.S. "Birkenhead," S.S. "Kotiti," S.S. "Kapanui," S.S. "Kawaii," "Waimarie" and "Taniwha," and also the well known cutter-yacht "Jessie Logan," and the celebrated yacht "Waitangi," now owned by a Wellington yachtsman, who has long annually come out first in the yacht races held at Port Nicholson.

Mr. R. Logan Sen

Lyne, Robert, was born in London in 1863 and travelled by the *Zealandia* in 1871 with his widowed mother. They settled at Hororata and when his uncle died in 1888 he succeeded to his property. He finished his education at Christ's College and was married in 1894 to Miss Prayer and they had one daughter in 1900.

Mr. R. R. Lyne

McLean, Alexander, was born in Ross-shire, Scotland and lived near Sir Hector McDonald who was a playmate of his as a child. Alexander came to Bluff on the *Zealandia* in December 1882. He started farming at Waimatuku, then Spar Bush, Waianiwa, where he lived until his death. He was connected with the Southland A. and P. Association, Caledonian Society, and Highland Society. He was Chief of the Highland Society at the time of his death in 1911.

Mason, George Dunsmore, was born in Perth Scotland and left with his parents in 1877 on the *Zealandia*. They were on board when the ship collided with and sank the *Ellen Lamb*. In 1880 George married Elizabeth Ann McLagan, in Blenheim where he was a watchmaker and jeweller. He spent five years in Blenheim and Reefton but the rest of his life in Wellington. He joined the Wellington Torpedo Corps in 1897 and retired in 1920 with the rank of Staff Artificer Quartermaster-Sergeant. He died in 1940, aged 86, and was survived by two daughters and two sons, with six grandchildren and one great grandchild.

Metcalf, Anthony, was a farmer at Wattle Hill Farm, Orari Bridge. He was born in 1846 in Stainwood, Westmorland, England and came to Lyttelton in 1869 on the *Zealandia*. He worked for six months for John Ruddenklau, then went sheep shearing by himself and was the first to start cropping on the Orari side of Geraldine. He had a trip home to England in 1875 on the ship *Rangitikei* and came home on the *Desdemona* the next year. He

Mr. A. Metcalf

was on the Geraldine Road Board and was a member of the Orari Bridge School Committee. He had a small stud of Leicesters imported by him from England. While in England he married Margaret Frances Sowerby of Barningham, Yorkshire and they had two sons and four daughters. He was also a Justice of the Peace.

Norton, John, was a Brick and Drain Pipe Manufacturer in Pukerau. He was born in Hallaton, Leicestershire and was brought up with brickmaking. He came to Port Chalmers on the *Zealandia* in 1875 and spent time at Dunedin and Roxburgh before settling at Chatton where he stayed until 1881. He then moved to Pukerau where he established his business. Mr. Norton was a member of the Cemetery Trustees, the Domain Board, and also of the Athenseum committee.

Mr. J. Norton

Parsons, Martha Spargo Bath, was born at Rilla Mill, Linkinhorne, Cornwall, the daughter of John and Catherine Nicholls. She arrived at Lyttelton in the ship *Zealandia* in 1871 and married in Timaru in 1872. They were pioneer farmers in the area. They then moved to Devonport. Mrs Parsons was a member of the Mother's Union for many years. She had nine children (seven of which survived), 11 grandchildren and three great grandchildren. She died aged 85 in 1935.

Radcliffe, William, was member of the Lyttelton Borough Council for many years. He was also the Mayor of Lyttelton for two years and four months and was in office when the "send-off" was given to the New Zealand Rough Riders. He was on many boards and committees. He was born in 1850 in the Isle of Man where he learned the trade of painter. He left on the *Zealandia* in 1870 arriving in Lyttelton. He lived in Lyttelton all his life except for five years spent on Banks Peninsula. In 1874 he became a house decorator and painter. He became a Justice of the Peace in 1896. Mr. Radcliffe was twice married; first, to a daughter of the late Mr. William Hollis and afterwards to the eldest daughter of the late Mr.

James Pitcaithly, of Pigeon Bay. He had a family of five children.

Reed, William, was the Proprietor of the Broadgate estate. He was born at Morchard-Bishop, Devonshire, England in 1846 and travelled on the *Zealandia* to Lyttelton in 1870. He went to Woodend and then bought land at Carleton near Oxford. He set up a business as a wheelwright and blacksmith at Saltwater Creek where he worked for two years. He then returned to Carleton and farmed there for over twenty years. He was a member of the Oxford Road Board. He married in England and they had a family of two sons and three daughters.

Mr. W. Reed

Rodgers, Mr. H. J., was a whole-sale Carpet, Linoleum and Linen Warehouseman, in Wellington. Mr. Rodgers was born in Wales, but went to Ireland when he was seven. He learnt his business in Limerick, and was apprenticed to the Limerick Warehouse Company. He completed his apprenticeship in 1875 and then worked as a journeyman. He travelled to Wellington on the *Zealandia* in 1879. For fifteen years Mr. Rodgers acted as manager of the carpet department of Te Aro House before moving to another business in 1893.

Russell, William, was a farmer at Hillside Farm, Gapes Valley. He was born in Forfarshire, Scotland in 1845 and came to New Zealand in 1872 on the *Zealandia*. He worked for three years farming at Maheno, North Otago and then moved to Canterbury. He cropped at Levels estate and then went to Waitohi where he leased land and worked for three years. He then bought Government land and farmed there for many years. He married at Maheno to Miss Proctor and they had five sons and three daughters.

***Sammons**, John,* was born in Oxfordshire, England in 1844. He went to sea as a youth and served 12 years in the Royal Navy, travelling around the world. He came to Bluff on the *Zealandia* in 1872 and joined the New Zealand Railway. He was guard until appointed officer in charge of Forest Hill Signal Station. He married in 1899.

Mr. J. Sammons

***Scott**, Mrs.,* travelled to Port Chalmers on the *Zealandia* in 1879. She married her husband in New Zealand and they celebrated their Golden Wedding in 1936 in Wellington. Mr Scott was into miniature rifle shooting. They had two sons and a daughter.

***Seybe**, Michael,* was a farmer at Wai-iti. He was born at Kindenheim, Germany in 1860 and travelled to New Zealand on the *Zealandia* arriving in Lyttelton in 1870. He settled in the Timaru district and was at Levels station for a few years. In 1898 he began farming 68 acres of land on the Wai-iti Road. He married in 1883 to the daughter of Mr. S. Morgan of Timaru and they had six sons and three daughters.

***Shaw**, Mr. Frederick,* was born in 1847 at Bourton-on-the-Water, Gloucestershire. He came to New Zealand in 1872 on the *Zealandia* and started work on railway formation for two and a half years. He entered the Government Railway service in 1880 as a ganger at Athol. He served on the Athol School Committee. He married in 1872 to a daughter of Mr. Jesse Lane, carpenter of Borton-on-the-water. They had four sons and five daughters and resided at Dipton.

***Skellings**, Mrs. James,* died at Riverside aged 73 in 1917. She had come to Lyttelton with her husband in the *Zealandia* in 1871. She was a much respected resident of Ashburton. Mr. and Mrs. Skellings lived at Kaiapoi and later Selwyn before finally settling at Ashburton. She was survived by her husband, four sons, four daughters, many grandchildren and great grandchildren.

Sherlock, William, was born in 1846 in London and came on the *Zealandia* to Lyttelton in 1872. He moved to Christchurch where he set up a business as a photographer for eighteen years. He settled on the West Coast in 1890 and set up a studio in Reefton.

Tubman, Mrs. Margaret, nee Kennedy (of County Cavan, Ireland) was a farmer at Moa Flat, Roxburgh. She owned 300 acres of freehold land and 1500 acres of leasehold land with 1000 sheep. She was the widow of Mr. Robert Tubman of North Ireland (born 1834) Mr. Tubman was interested in mining and joined the Miner's Association and local school committee. Mr. and Mrs. Tubman married in 1875. Mrs. Tubman came to New Zealand on the *Zealandia* in 1870.

Mr. R. Tubman & eldest son

Tucker, Joshua, was a well known figure in Ashburton. He came to New Zealand on the *Zealandia* with brother Caleb Tucker in 1871. He was very well respected and "his word was his bond." He served on local bodies. In his obituary it stated, "No man will be more missed than he from the everyday life of the community." He was born in 1845 at North Molton, Devonshire. After arriving in New Zealand he worked on the land for two years and then joined coal merchants where he was appointed manager, eventually taking over the business himself. Mr Tucker gave long and valuable service on public bodies in Ashburton. The number of boards he belonged to was almost too great to list. He married in 1871 to Miss Maynard, daughter of Captain Maynard of Redruth. They had seven children. His wife died and he married again to Miss Jameson. They had one son. Joshua died in 1921 at Allenton aged 75 years old.

Victor, James, was an officer on the *Zealandia* when it came out to New Zealand in 1871. On the return journey Captain White was swept overboard. Victor's obituary doesn't fit with the original story of the terrible return journey where he claims the first mate, himself and several of the passengers and crew were washed overboard. Mr Victor himself was apparently washed back on board and took the vessel to safety receiving much praise! This we fear is nothing but a yarn spun to his family, who then quoted it to the newspapers on his death. James came back to New Zealand and joined the Railway. He was a foreman of the goods department at Christchurch and then became a teacher. He made several trips to South Africa and Australia. He left a widow, two sons and four daughters when he died in 1907.

Winder, George, was a well known Wellington ironmonger who had his business on the corner of Cuba Street and Manners Street. He was born in County Clare, Ireland and travelled to Wellington in 1879 on the *Zealandia*. He worked for others for 11 years before establishing his own business. He was a member of the Wellington Bowling Club, and was a Master Mason in the New Zealand Pacific Lodge. He retired, had a trip abroad and returned to Wellington, dying in 1930.

Mr. George Winder

Passenger Lists

1869

London 18 August 1869 – Lyttelton 20 November 1869

Name		Age	Location	Occupation
Chief Cabin				
Foulger	Rev. J.			
Horston	Mr. G. A.			
Fowell	Mr. G.			
Mersons	Miss Hester			
Turnbull	Mr. Thomas			
Turnbull	Miss Kate			
Wood	Mr. James			
George	Mr. S.			
Adams	Mrs.			
Brouncker	Mr. William			
Karslake	Mr. W.W.C.			
Bray	Mr. W. B.			
Bray	Family (3)			
Hutchison	Mr.			
Hutchison	Mrs.			
Strouts	Mr.			
Strouts	Family (4)			
Strouts	Servant			
Second Cabin				
Mann	James			
Mann	Mrs.			
Moore	Miss E.			
Digby	J.R.B.			
Digby	Family (4)			
Kingdon	Charles F.			
Kennedy	James			
Andrews	James			
Souter	William			

Gay	Miss H.			
Third class				
Unknown (20)				

1870

London 23 September 1870 – Lyttelton 23 December 1870

Name		Age	Location	Occupation
Chief Cabin				
Biggs	Miss L. G.			
Bradley	Miss E. C.			
Whincop	Mr A.			
Whincop	Mrs M.			
Crow	Captain C.S.			
Crow	Mrs E.M.			
Broadfoot	Mr Alex.			
Broadfoot	Mrs H.K.			
Somerville	Mr R.J.			
Thatteris	Mr Henry			
Forrall/Turrell	Mr Walter E.			
Pascoe	Mr W.A.			
Saunders	Mr F.D.			
Benn	Mr William H.			
Benn	Mr S.J.			
Benn	Mr John			
De Lapasteur	Mr Henry P.			
Batt	Dr C.D.			
Steerage				
Abbott	Mary	22		General servant
Ahlers	Helena	24		General servant
Arras	Wilhelm	19		Farm labourer
Arthur	George	22		Farm labourer
Arthur	Ann	18		

Passenger Lists

Surname	Given	Age		Occupation
Beesley	Maria	27		Cook
Borland	James	40		Sadler
Borland	Emma	33		
Borland	Maggie	16		Nurserymaid
Borland	Robert	10		
Borland	Emma	8		
Borland	William	6		
Borland	Charles	5		
Borland	Sarah	3		
Borland	John	4m		
Bourne	John	22		Farm labourer
Bourne	Fanny	24		
Bourne	Edith	4		
Breeze	Matthew	40		Farm labourer
Breeze	John	20		Farm labourer
Brown	Francis	49		Ploughman
Brown	Sarah	40		
Brown	Daniel	21		Clerk
Brown	Sarah	20		Dairymaid
Brown	Jessie	18		General servant
Brown	Francis	16		Farm labourer
Brown	Alexander	14		
Brown	William	6		
Brown	Jane	4		
Calder	William	20		Ploughman
Caldwell	Thomas	24		Ploughman
Callaghan	John	20		Farm labourer
Campbell	Flora	22		Dairymaid
Campbell	Margaret	18		Dairymaid
Canavan	George	25		Labourer
Carroll				Matron to ship
Chick	Peter	22		Farm labourer
Christie	Ann	19		Nurserymaid
Clark	Ann	60		

Passenger Lists

Corbet	Euphemia	24		General servant
Corkery	John	20		Farm labourer
Cowbrick	Sydney	26		Coachmaker
Cowbrick	Clara	21		
Cross	Eliza	27		Cook
Cutler	Alice	26		
Cutler	Thomas	26		Forgeman
Davies	Benjamin	38		Moulder
Davies	Elizabeth	37		
Dermott	James	22		Farm labourer
Dick	Mary Ann	23		General servant
Dyer	Martha	38		
Dyer	Emily	16		General servant
Dyer	Amelia	15		General servant
Esselborn	Maria	22		General servant
Evans	Edward	29		Carpenter & C
Evans	Richard	26		Farm labourer
Evans	Martha M.	21		
Evans	Rowland	17		Ploughman
Evans	Fanny K.	3		
Fawkes	Caroline M.	20		General servant
Fell	Josiah	27		Farm labourer
Fell	Elizabeth	27		
Fell	Infant			
Forrest	Cathy J.	29		Housemaid
Fourdrinier	Alfred	23		Labourer
Gamble	Charles	20		Farm labourer
Gilbert	John	35		Millwright
Gilbert	Caroline	34		
Gilbert	Arthur	9m		
Gilbert	Henry	7		
Gilbert	Emma	4		
Green	Samuel	28		Farm labourer
Green	Mary	27		

Passenger Lists

Green	Clara	6		
Green	Jessie	4		
Green	Kate	2		
Green	Annie	1		
Griebel [Griebell]	Peter	28		Farm labourer
Griebel [Griebell]	Maria	22		Dairymaid
Griffiths	Mary	51		
Griffiths	John	50		Farm labourer
Griffiths	Hannah	26		
Griffiths	John (jnr)	24		farm labourer
Griffiths	Mary (jnr)	20		General servant
Griffiths	Sarah	16		General servant
Griffiths	Samuel	11		
Griffiths	John James	1		
Grutel	Jakobine	28		Dairymaid
Gudex	Magdalena	20		Dairymaid
Gutel	Jakobine	28		Dairymaid
Haeslip	John	26		Labourer
Haines	Michael	44		Farm labourer
Haines	Ruth	42		
Hardwick	John	42		Farm labourer
Hardwick	Hannah	42		
Hardwick	Elizabeth	4m		
Hardwick	Thomas	17		Farm labourer
Hardwick	John	14		
Hardwick	William	11		
Hardwick	Mary	9		
Hardwick	Catherine	6		
Hardwick	Amy	3		
Harris	Jane	24		General servant
Harris	William	20		Farm labourer
Hayler	James	34		Farm labourer
Hayler	Mary A.	26		
Hayler	James	7		

Hayler	Sarah	1		
Henwood	Thomas	28		Farm labourer
Henwood	Emma	27		
Hicks	Henry	24		Farm labourer
Hicks	Mary	19		
Hollobon	Mary	40		
Hollobon	Alfred	16		Tinman
Hollobon	Albert	13		
Hollobon	Jesse	10		
Hollobon	Arthur	5		
Hollobon	Emily	4		
Hollobon	Ellen	2		
Houghton	Katherine	17		Domestic servant
Huffey	George	35		Coachman
Hutchinson	Jane	21		General servant
James	Matilda	16		General servant
Johns	Albert R.	7m		
Johns	William	36		Farm labourer
Johns	Mary	35		
Johns	W. Henry	16		Labourer
Johns	John James	11		
Johns	George Thomas	8		
Johns	Mary A.	6		
Johns	Jessie	3		
Jones	Mary	34		General servant
Jones	Jane	16		General servant
Jones	Minnie	9		
Jones	William	4		
Joyce	Mary	25		General servant
Leary	John	22		Farm labourer
Leary	Catherine	21		Dairymaid
Leary	William	19		Farm labourer
Leary	Ellen	16		Dairymaid
Mayn	Emma	30		

Mayn	James	30		Farm labourer
Mayn	Mary J.	11		
Mayn	John	10		
Mayn	James	7		
Mayn	Emma	5		
Mayn	Elizabeth A.	2		
McNae	Richard	48		Engineer
McNae	Ann	21		General servant
Miller	Jane	26		General servant
Milne	Jessie	3m		
Morcombe	Mary	30		General servant
Morgans	John	21		Farm labourer
Morgans	Edward	18		Farm labourer
Moyle	James	28		Farm labourer
Moyle	William	21		Farm labourer
Munro	John William	23		Shepherd
Murphy	Patrick	27		Labourer
Murphy	Margaret	21		General servant
Nicholls	Martha	19		General servant
Norman	Richard L.	20		Boilermaker
Nott	John	18		Ploughman
Osborn	Josh Richard	26		Labourer
Page	Eliza	48		
Page	John	48		Labourer
Page	Frederick	19		Ploughman
Page	William	19		Labourer
Page	Eliza Jane	12		
Page	Harry	6		
Page	James	5		
Patton	Johan			General servant
Patton	Thomas	30		Ploughman
Patton	Elizabeth	22		Dairymaid
Poff	Johanna	22		General servant
Pound	Emma	27		General servant

Passenger Lists

Power	Elizabeth	24		General servant
Power	George	22		Gardener
Rainbow	James	37		Farm labourer
Rainbow	Caroline	36		
Rainbow	Henry S.	15		Farm labourer
Reed	Mary Ann	24		
Reed	William	23		Smith
Richards	William	30		Farm labourer
Robertson	Alexandria	21		General servant
Russell	Anne	26		General servant
Scott	Mary	61		General servant
Seager	Mary A.	54		
Seager	Samuel H.	50		Carpenter
Seager	Rose	18		Domestic servant
Seager	Samuel	15		Labourer
Seager	Jane	13		
Seager	Ada	11		
Seib	Michael	20		Farm labourer
Shea	Dennis	24		Farm labourer
Simpson	John	47		Ploughman
Simpson	Jane	45		
Simpson	Martha	40		
Simpson	George	36		Farm labourer
Simpson	Mary	20		General servant
Simpson	Henry	10		
Simpson	Martha	7		
Simpson	Frederick	4		
Spillane	Thomas	26		Farm labourer
Stewart	Kate	10		
Stuart	Selina	26		Housekeeper
Stuart	Frances A.	6½y		
Sullivan	Cornelius	22		Labourer
Swann	Lucy	3		
Timpson	Charlotte	25		Cook

Tudor	David	35		Farm labourer
Webb	Thomas	59		Farm labourer
Webb	Sarah	57		
Webb	Emma	19		general servant
Willis	Lewis	35		Shepherd
Willis	Christina	32		
Wise	George	29		Farm labourer
Wise	Ellen	22		
Wise	George R.	4m		
Wotten	David	21		Farm labourer
Yates	John	23		Labourer

1871

London 8 September 1871 – Lyttelton 9 December 1871

Name		Age	Location	Occupation
Families and children				
Allen	John	30	Montgomery	Farm labourer
	Elizabeth	22		
	John	1		
Berrill	Thomas	63	Bedfordshire	Bricklayer
	Ann	63		
Brosnan	Timothy	39	Kerry	Farm labourer
	Kate	36		
	Kate	17	Trans to single women	
	Mary	15	Trans to single women	
	Timothy	11		
	Hugh	7		
	Patrick	5		
	Bridget	2		
	John	Infant		
Carter	Bevis W.	30	Somersetshire	Farm labourer
	Elizabeth J.	26		
Corbett	Thomas	55	Down	Farm labourer
	Eliza J.	53		
	Thomas	21	Trans to single men	

Passenger Lists

	Mary A.	18	Trans to single women	
	Eliza Jane	15	Trans to single women	
Gallagher	Robert	28	Tyrone	Farm labourer
	Eliza	27		
	Martha	9		
	William	5		
	Robert	3		
Glanville	James	30	Cornwall	Carpenter
	Ann	33		
	Ann	63		
Hutchinson	Edward	39	Kildare	Ploughman
	Margaret	28		
	Sarah	7		
	Alice	5		
	Margaret	4		
	Ellen	2		
Kenzie	William	50	Morayshire	Farm labourer
	Isabella	50		
	Matilda	22	Trans to single women	
	Isabella	18	Trans to single women	
	Wilhelmina	16	Trans to single women	
Manhire	William	60	Cornwall	Miner
	Elizabeth	58		
	Naomi	24	Trans to single women	
	Jemima	19	Trans to single women	
Marsh	William Edward	26	Devonshire	Cook
	Mary L.	25		
	Edward W	2		
	Elizabeth	58	Trans to single women	
Rimmington	William H.	10		Travelling with marsh's
	Ann	9		Travelling with marsh's
Mccausland	William	52	Tyrone	Farm labourer
	Mary	40		
	Clark	20	Trans to single men	
	James	18	Trans to single men	
	Alexander	16	Trans to single men	
Mole	Josiah	35	Worcestershire	Labourer
	Hannah	28		
	Emma C.	7		
Newman	George	27	Hants	Farm labourer
	Thirza	24		

Passenger Lists

Palmer	William	43	Yorkshire	Gardener
	Catherine	42		
Scaife	John	44	Yorkshire	Farm labourer
	Jane	32		
	Kate	8		
	Mary	7		
	Ada	5		
	Rachel A.	3		
	William	1		
Scott	William	35	Lancashire	Foundryman
	Emma	36		
	Elizabeth	11		
	Mary	9		
	John	7		
	William	5		
	Louisa	2		
Skilling	James	24	Ayr	Ploughman
	Helen	25		
	Mary	3		
	William	1		
Tucker	Joshua	25	Devonshire	Farm labourer
	Mary E.	21		
Westaway	Thomas	29	Cornwall	Farm labourer
	Elizabeth	26		
Whitford	Joseph	29	Cornwall	Farm labourer
	Mary	27		
	Mary	4		
	Rosina	7 mths		
Worboys	John N.	28	Middlesex	Painter
	Eliza	30		
	Joshua H.	5		
Single men				
Baker	Charles W.	20	Devonshire	Farm labourer
	John W.	22	Devonshire	Farm labourer
Barnes	Philip	24	Cornwall	Farm labourer
Berry	Daniel	51	Middlesex	Bricklayer
	Henry	14		
	Edward	11		
Berry	William	27	Middlesex	Bricklayer & brickmaker
	Daniel	25	Middlesex	Bricklayer and brickmaker

Corbett	Thomas	21	Down	Ploughman
	Joseph	23	Down	Ploughman
Crompton	James	17	Yorkshire	Farm labourer
Cullen	Joseph	23	Wexford	Labourer
Dennison	William	23	Down	Farm labourer
Everiss	George	29	Glostershire	Schoolmaster on board
Finlay	John	17	Wicklow	Farm labourer
Graham	James	21	Down	Ploughman
Hardie	Walter	28	Somersetshire	Labourer
Haskett	Henry	18	Tipperary	Harness maker
Hughes	Edward L.	24	Pembrokeshire	Farm labourer
Knox	John	24	Down	Farm labourer
Mccausland	Clark	20	Tyrone	Farm labourer
	James	18	Tyrone	Farm labourer
	Alexander	16	Tyrone	Farm labourer
Mcdonald	Rodeerick	23	Inverness	Shepherd
Parsons	Charles	30	Dorset	Labourer
Poff	James	22	Kerry	Farm labourer
Quinton	William	22	Suffolk	Labourer
Smith	Frederick	39	Hants	Farm labourer
Somerville	Thomas	21	Tyrone	Farm labourer
Tanguey	Michael	24	Kerry	Tailor
Tucker	Caleb	19	Devonshire	Farm labourer
Vivian	William John	22	Cornwall	Farm labourer
Single women				
Appleby	Mary	29	Wicklow	General servant
Barnaby	Arenea M.	21	Kent	Cook
Beal	Mary	21	Worchestershire	General servant
Bells	Mary Ann	20	Buckinghamshire	General servant
Berry	Eliza	17	Middlesex	General servant
Brady	Mary	26	Down	General servant
Brosnan	Kate	17	Kerry	General servant
	Mary	15	Kerry	General servant
Butler	Johanna	18	Kerry	General servant
Clarke	Sarah	33	Suffolk	
	Arthur	7 mths		
Cochrane	Jane	26	Ayr	General servant
	Annie	22	Ayr	General servant
	Helen	52	Ayr	General servant
Corbett	Mary A.	18	Down	Cook
	Eliza J.	15	Down	General servant

Passenger Lists

Surname	First Name	Age	County	Occupation
Crimmen	Ellen	22	Kerry	General servant
Gethin	Annie	37	Glamorgan	General servant
	Hannah	16	Glamarogan	General servant
Fenton	Elizabeth	23	Antrim	General servant
Harris	Ellen	17	Devon	General servant
Haskett	Anne	16	Tipperary	General servant
Hawker	Ann	38	Berkshire	Matron
Hooper	Harriet	19	Cornwall	General nurse
Johnson	Alice	16	Middlesex	General servant
Kelson	Elizabeth	22	Somerset	General servant
Lawrence	Mary A.	27	Middlesex	Cook
Lynes	Hannah	29	Bucks	Laundress
	Elizabeth	11		
	Robert	7		
Manhire	Naomi	24	Cornwall	General servant
	Jemima	19	Cornwall	General servant
Marsh	Elizabeth	58	Devonshire	
Mckenzie	Matilda	22	Aberdeen	General servant
	Isabella	18	Aberdeen	
	Wilhelmina	16	Aberdeen	General servant
Parsons	Mary L.	16	Berks	General servant
Proud	Janet	27	Durham	Nurse
Renolds	Susannah	17	Middlesex	General servant
Sarchet	Emma P.	36	Guernsey	General servant
	Patty E.	36	Guernsey	General servant
Scollard	Mary	21	Kerry	General servant
Shrempf	Caroline	15	America	
	Annie	10	America	
Simpson	George ?	21	Middlesex	Nurse
Sommerville	Margaret	20	Tyrone	General servant
	Mary	24	Tyrone	General servant
Stevenson	Agnes	21	Down	Dairymaid
Summers	Jane	19	Sussex	Housemaid
Wall	Honora	20	Galway	Dairymaid
Whicker	Henrietta C.	19	Devonshire	General servant
Whitnell	Mary A.	16	Devonshire	General servant
Wilson	Sarah A.	31	Norfolk	Cook
Williams	Martha	28	Montgomery	Cook
Yeomanson	Hannah	22	Kent	Cook

1872

London 8 October 1872 – Bluff 28 December 1872 & Port Chalmers 4 January 1873

Name		Age	County	Occupation/ Notes
Bluff passengers	(28 Dec 1872)			
Silvester	Alfred			
Silvester	Mary Anne			
Silvester	Charles			
Stewart	David			
Stewart	Mrs			
McLean	Alexander			
Fahy	Kate			
Kearney	Honor			
Young	Margaret			
Unknown	For Messrs Brogden (184)			
Port Chalmers	**(4 Jan 1873)**			
Blarney	Mr. J.			
Blarney	Mrs.			
Blarney	Children (2)			
Williams	Miss			
Digby	Mr. P. J.			
Rhodes	Mr. D. R.			
Rhodes	Hiram			
Port Chalmers Steerage				
Cormack	Donald	60	Caithness	Farrier
	Mary	50		Wife
	Benjamin	21	T/F Single Men	Ploughman
Taylor	John	40	Caithness	Ploughman
	Elizabeth	28		Wife
McIntyre	Donald	22	Sutherland	Shepherd
	Annie	23		
Neal	William	26	Stafford	Gardener
	Elizabeth	28		
Knox	Henry	32	Cavan	Labourer
	Mary	30		
	Wm. Thomas	10		
	Annie J.	8		
	Henry	4		
	Jno. James	8 mths		
Culbert	William	30	Donegal	Farm Servant
	Janet	25		
	James	5		
	Ann	3		
	William	10 mth		
Cockburn	John	53	Berwickshire	Farm Labourer
	Elizabeth	47		Wife

Passenger Lists

	Euphemia	20	T/F Single Women	Gl. Servant	
	David	17	T/F Single Men		
	John	12	T/F Single Men		
	Robert	10			
	Sarah	8			
Stewart	David	33	Perthshire	Labourer	
	Mrs.	41		Wife	
Brown	John	38	Fife	Labourer	
	Elizabeth	36		Wife	
	John	17	T/F Single Men	Baker	
	Jane	15	T/F Single Women	Servant	
	William	13			
	James	11			
	Peter	9			
	Andrew	3			
	Agnes	11 mth			
Single Men					
Cormack	Benjamin	21	Caithness	Ploughman	
Pierce	William	20	Fermarnagh	Ag Labourer	
Russell	William	28	Forfarshire	Ploughman	
McLean	Alexander	21	Rosshire	Farm Servant	
Cockburn	David	17	Berwickshire	Farm Labourer	
Cockburn	John	12	Berwickshire	Farm Labourer	
Kennedy	John	24	Cavan	Farm Labourer	
Argue	Thomas	50	Cavan	Gardener	
Argue	Mary Ann	28	T/F Single Women	Nurse	
Argue	William	25	Cavan	Coachman	
Mooney	Patrick	19	Armagh	Farm Servant	
Crawford	John	22	Fermarnagh	Farm Servant	
Cronis or Ernis	Christopher	22	Dublin	Tailor	
Urquhart	William	28	Inverness	Farm Labourer	
Kinnaird	William	15	Ayr	Farm Labourer	
Sinclair	Barnelson	20	Caithness	Shoemaker	
Dale	Mark R.	15	York		
Dale	James	20	York	Joiner	
Brown	John	17	Fife	Baker	
Brown	William	13	Fife		
Single Women					
Bourke	Elizabeth	24	Mayo	Laundress	
Murphy	Ellen	26	Galway	Gl. Servant	
Dale	Eliza A.	48	Yorks	Charwoman	
Hancock	Selina	35	Middlesex	Matron	
Bryant	Elizabeth	23	Longford	Cook	
Kennedy	Margaret	22	Cavan	Cook	
Dale	Sarah A.	17	York	Nurse	
Pratt	Charlotte	42	Suffolk	Laundress	
Pratt	Annie Maria	4			
Pratt	Charlotte	6			
Price	Ellen	53	Sussex	Laundress	
Humphreys	Louisa	18	Middlesex	Dom. Servant	
Guinnell	Julia J.	28	Gloucestershire	Dom. Servant	
Graham	Fanny	30	Fermanagh		

Graham	Mary	6		
Graham	Samuel	4		
Graham	Lizzie	2		
Graham	Fanny	22	Fermanagh	Genl. Servant
McCann	Susanna	23	Tyrone	Servant
McAleer	Mary	17	Tyrone	Servant
Donnelly	Mary	18	Tyrone	Servant
Galway	Elizabeth	26	Carlow	Dairymaid
Fahy	Kate	27	Galway	Servant
Eagan	Julia	18	Galway	Servant
Jordan	Mary	25	Galway	Servant
Jordan	Bridget	23	Galway	Servant
Forde	Bridget	23	Galway	Servant
Moylan	Mary	20	Galway	Servant
Heaney	Honour	19	Galway	Servant
Paul	Agnes	46	Renfrewshire	Servant
Paul	Janet	13	Renfrewshire	Servant
Young	Margaret	28	Perthshire	Housemaid
Manning	Sarah	28	Surrey	
Manning	Louise	5		
Manning	Percy G.	3		
Hauly	Bridget	21	Tipperary	Servant
Hauly	Judith	19	Tipperary	Servant
Holmes	Alice M.	20	Gloucestershire	Cook
Greenslade	Lavinia	20	Devon	Gl. Servant
McLean	Catherine	24	Inverness	Gl. Servant
Lunn	Elizabeth	20	Edinburgh	Cook
Lunn	Jessie	24	Edinburgh	Housemaid

1873

London 29 August 1873 – Port Chalmers 29 November 1873

Name		Age	County	Occupation/Notes
Saloon				
Raynor	Mr.			
Raynor	Mrs.			
Tolson	Mr.			
Tolson	Mrs.			
Tolson	Family (5)			
Dodd	Mr.			
Dodd	Mrs.			
Shearman	Mrs			
Preston	Miss W.			
Nicholl	Miss			
Barker	Messrs (2)			
Burben	Mr.			
Anderson	Mr.			

Passenger Lists

Duncan	Mr.			
Deires	Mr.			
Travis	Mr.			
Pizzie	Mr.			
Hudson	Mr.			
Steerage				
Families and Children				
Dawson	Benjamin	38	Lancashire	Gardener
	Ann	37		
Sansom	James	23	Dorset	Quarryman
	Elizabeth	22		
Crook	Thomas	39	Wiltshire	Tailor
	Honoria	34		
	Samuel T	11		
Stuart	George	28	Banffshire	Tailor
	Annie	22		
	Caroline	9 mth		
Owens	John	21	Montgomeryshire	Collier
	Jane	22		
Drees	Henry	52	Germany	Tailor
	Susan	51		
	Henry	18	T/F Single Men	Tailor
	Caroline	11		
Faith	Thomas	27	Middlesex	Tailor
	Elizabeth	26		
Hardie	Jonathan P.	44	Jersey	Tailor
	Mary A.	35		
	John J.	12	T/F Single Men	
	Charles D.	10		
	Mary A.	8		
Hellion	Francis	35	Jersey	Shoemaker
	Angel	26		
	Margaret A.	6		
	Francis P.	5		
	Mary L.	2		
Alger	Edward	29	Norfolk	Tailor
	Mary A.	32		
	Charle	2		
	Agnes	4		
	Elizabeth	2 mth		
Gill	Samuel	38	Yorks	Labourer
	Sarah	36		
	Mary J.	13	T/F Single Women	
	Sarah A.	9		
Le Brus	Yoes M.	25	Jersey	Gardener
	Jean M.	24		
	Jean L. M.	2		
Jennings	Frederick	34	Cambridge	Tailor
	Anne	29		
Le Irony	Paul	30	Jersey	Carpenter

Passenger Lists

	Marie	30		
	Melanie	1		
Humphreys	Frederick	33	Surrey	Gl. Labourer
	Charlotte	28		
	Frederick	9		
Spriggs	William	42	Northampton	Platelayer
	Eliza	35		
	William	13	T/F Single Men	
Illingworth	Robert	34	Yorks	Mechanic
	Mary J.	35		
	Alice	7		
	Alfred	5		
	Willie	1		
Burford	Thomas	29	Suffolk	Tailor
	Mary	20		
	Alice	2		
	Alfred	3 mth		
Sanson	George J.	33	Dorsetshire	Quarrymen
	Mary	28		
	Mary	9		
	George Thomas	6		
	Robert F.	4		
	Priscilla J.	1		
Hoskins	William	33	Dorset	Quarryman
	Harriet	31		
	William Henry	12	T/F Single Men	
	Robert	9		
	Henry	7		
	Thomas	4		
Moulain	Joseph	27	Yorks	Carpenter
	Hannah	21		
Cole	Thomas	29	Gloucestershire	Carpenter
	Jane	30		
	Mary E.	3		
	Tom T.	18 mth		
Krake	Frederick	30	Germany	Tailor
	Eliza	31		
	Helly	3		
	Frederic	11 mth		
Webb	Samuel	33	Middlesex	Tailor
	Maria	32		
	Alice	7		
	Samuel	4		
	Catherine	10 mth		
Loder	William	25	Warwick	Carpenter
	Martha	29		
Stokes	John	24	Hunts	Labourer

Passenger Lists

	Elizabeth	20		
	Jane E.	10 mth		
Moulin	Francois	22	Jersey	Baker
	Susan	22		
Lock	George William	39	Guernsey	Iron Founder
	Elizabeth	40		
	George	18	T/F Single Men	Labourer
	Charles D.	17	T/F Single Men	
	Thomas	13	T/F Single Men	
Wohlers	John	27	Germany	Tailor
	Emma	22		
	Albert	2		
	Sophy	8 mth		
Proudford	Richard	28	Waterford	Tailor
	Mary A.	27		
	Alice	3		
	Richard	9 mth		
	Eliza	2		
Rushworth	John	34	Yorks	Engine Driver
	Martha	30		
	Anne	1		
Dufton	Jules	27	Belgium	Tailor
	Robena	29		
Ransome	Henry	36	Yorks	Tailor
	Emily G. A.	30		
	Blanche E.	5		
Stokes	William	34	Surrey	Carpenter
	Matilda	34		
	Frederic	11		
	Harriet	8		
	Alice	6		
	Ellen	3		
	Lilly	16 mth		
Chandler	William Henry	29	Hants	Farm Labourer
	Annie	26		
Lapper	Michael	27	Armagh	Tailor
	Frances	23		
	Sarah	2		
Owld	James	40	Cornwall	Baker
	Margaret	35		
	Ada	9		
	Matilda	7		
	James	4		
Grobarth	August	40	Germany	Tailor
	Jessie	32		
	Edward	6 mth		
Lockwood	Henry	45	Cambridgeshire	Tailor
	Emma	46		

Passenger Lists

	Emma	18	T/F Single Women	Tailoress
	Henry	16	T/F Single Men	Tailor
	John	13	T/F Single Men	
	Eliza	13	T/F Single Men	
	Alice	8		
Waller	August	32	Germany	Tailor
	Sarah	25		
	Hannah E.	3		
Holliday	William	34	Lancashire	Tailor
	Edith	32		
Baxter	John	37	Yorks	Joiner
	Mary A.	35		
	Walter	10		
	Albert Ed.	6		
	Jonathan William	2		
Grasby	William	28	Yorks	Joiner
	Emma	32		
Muller	Angus	31	Denmark	Tailor
	Emily	37		
Burnett	Henry	23		
	Ann	22		
Roberts	Ellis	28	Denbighshire	Collier
	Catherine	25		
Stevens	Jonathan R.	46	Suffolk	Waterman
	Sarah J.	31		
	Jonathan R.	10		
	Henry C.	3		
Single Men				
Keenan	Patrick	23	Westmeath	Farm Labourer
Davies	John	20	Cardiganshire	Collier
Goold	Frederic	20	Norfolk	Tailor
Toogood	William	24	Wiltshire	Gardener
Barker	William P.	23	Yorks	Labourer
Thomas	Benjamin	22	Pembrokeshire	Collier
Butterfield	Daniel	21	Surrey	Tailor
Stephens	William B.	19	Jersey	Carpenter
Morrish	William J.	32	Devon	Tailor
Lyon	Sidney J.	22	Pembrokeshire	Tailor
Watershouse	Jonathan	22	Lancashire	Tailor
Mallard	William	21	Berkshire	Tailor
Stewart	James	21	Cambridgeshire	Whitesmith
Smith	Frederick	21	Cambridge	Tailor
Cassell	Henry T.	32	Middlesex	
Thomas	David	23	Carmarthanshire	
Lowen	William Ed.	21	Essex	Labourer
Dunster	John	25	Surrey	Tailor
Gilbert	William	26	Cornwall	Farm Labourer
Ede	James W.	29	Cornwall	Farm Labourer
Gale	George	29	Kent	Tailor
Hamer	Richard	31	Montgomery	Collier

James	William	28	Carmarthenshire	Collier
Evans	Daniel	27	Pembrokeshire	
Kearns	Jonathan George	19	Surrey	Carpenter
Fisher	William	30	Berkshire	Labourer
Mainwaring	Edward	26	Glamorganshire	Collier
Rowlands	David	25	Monmouthshire	
Goodger	Matthew	22	New Zealand	Groom
Maddy	Thomas	28	Brecon	Collier
Crutchfield	William	36	Berkshire	Labourer
Shortel	Matthew	22	Kilkenny	Farm Labourer
Single Women				
O'Halloran	Maria	15	Clare	Servant
Stokes	Emma	19	Hunts	Servant
Andrews	Julia	19	Herts	Servant
Daborn	Ada	22	Surrey	Servant
Eddy	Margaret	21	Jersey	Servant
Lorman	Fanny	25	Middlesex	Cook
Kaufmann	Ann	19	Germany	Servant
Feltham	Mary	33	Somerset	Dairymaid and Matron on board ship
Donollan	Margaret	20	Clare	Gl. Servant
Harris	Leah	20	Pembrokeshire	Dressmaker
Le Brocq	Eliza E.	30	Jersey	Servant
Williams	Rachel	18	Glamorganshire	Servant
Williamson	Rohia	29	Orkney	Farm Servant
Williamson	Agnes	8		
Robinson	Mary	19	Lancashire	Housemaid
O'Halloran	Margaret	18	Clare	Servant
Giles	Harriet	33	Hants	
Giles	Andrew G.	9		
Giles	Elizabeth E.	7		
Giles	Henry James	4		
Driscoll	Ann	26	Cork	Servant
Egleton	Anne P.	23	Forfarshire	Seamstress

1875

London 17 July 1875 – Port Chalmers 27 October 1875

Name		*Age*	*County*	*Occupation/Notes*
Cabin Passengers				
Pearde	Mrs.			
Young	Mr.			
Baldwin	Mr.			
Monkhome	Mr.			
Second Cabin				
Unknown (7)				
Free and Colonial Nominated Immigrants in Steerage				

Passenger Lists

Families and Children				
Crosley	Michael	28	Durham	Brickmaker
	Jane	24		
Collett	Thomas	29	Gloucestershire	Joiner
	Lucy A.	35		
	Mildred L.	3		
	Clara E.			
Henderson	Andrew	33	Down	Farm Labourer
	Alice	29		
	John	12	T/F single men	
	James	9		
	Alice	6		
	Joseph	3		
	Mary	11 Mth		
Ingram	John	27	Essex	Labourer
	Eliza	25		
	John	4		
	William	1		
Horne	Frederick	44	Middlesex	Tailor
	Laura	38		
	Ellen	19	T/F Single women	Pupil Teacher
	Marion	19	T/F Single women	Machinist
	Frederick	14	T/F single men	
	Charles	11		
	Laura	9		
	Florence	3		
	Linford	75	T/F single men	
Johnson	Peter	48	Norway	Sailmaker
	Mary	31		
	Mary A.	16	T/F single women	
McCarthy	Cornelia	34	Middlesex	Smith
	Mary	31		
Mitchell	Edward	38	Cornwall	Saddler
	Frances A.	30		
	Elizabeth A.	32	T/F Single women	Servant
Suinard	Nathaniel	36	Sussex	Painter Dc
	Caroline	33		
	Charles	11		
	Emma	10		
Tingey	Joseph	31	Middlesex	Painter Dc
	Elizabeth	31		
	Florence C.	5 mths		
Wardle	Jonathan R.	29	Northumberland	Stone Mason
	Jane	27		
	Robert R.	2		
	Elizabeth	56	T/F Single women	
Dalley	Andrew	30	Worcestershire	Smith
	Eliza A.	33		
	Andrew	8		

Passenger Lists

	James	mths		
Dring	Allan	24	Oxon	Labourer
	Susan	21		
Harvey	Robert	33	Norfolk	Carpenter
	Hephzibah	34		
	Thomas H.	7		
	Claude H.	3		
	Jessie M.	1 3/4 yrs		
Kempster	William	28	Herts	Farm Labourer
	Elizabeth	28		
McElhinny	Michael	25	Donegal	Farm Labourer
	Mary	27		
	Eliza	3		
	Michael	1 mth		
Hegarty	Catherine	25	T/F Single Women	Servant (Travelled with McElhinny)
Quarterman	George	39	Oxon	Farmer
	Emma	37		
	Edward	18	T/F Single Men	
	Emma	16	T/F Single women	
	George	14	T/F Single men	
	William	12	T/F single men	
	Seymour	8		
	Frederick	6		
	Linda	4		
	Arthur	3 mths		
Thow	Andrew	33	Forfar	Farm Labourer
	Wilhelmina	28		
Walker	James	28	Lanarkshire	Bricklayer
	Margaret	24		
	Isabella	4		
	Hugh	2 1/2		
	Margaret	1		
Clemo	William Henry	29	Cornwall	Cabinet Maker
	Ann	29		
Mayhew	Robert	30	Sulfolk	Cabinet Maker
	Catherine E.	28		
	Harriet B.	5		
	Elizabeth A.	4		
	Louisa	16 mths		
Thunley	John	26	lancashire	Pointsman
	Sarah A.	24		
	Clara E.	5		
	Ethel M.	3		
Broughton	Theodore	25	T/F single men	Travelled with Thunley
Vaughan	John	25	Cork	Labourer
	Julia	23		
	John	3		

Passenger Lists

	Mary	1		
Clarke	William Joseph	33	Suffolk	Printer
	Elizabeth Y.?	32		
	Richard J.	12	T/F Single Men	
	Elizabeth H.	11		
	Albert C.	6		
	William Joseph	2		
	Wm. Alfred	3 mths		
Pollock	John	40	Dumbarton	Joiner
	Hannah	40		
	Jane	21	T/F Single women	Servant
	Christine	19	T/F Single Women	Servant
	Duncan	17	T/F Single Men	
	John	12	T/F Single Men	
	Mary	10		
	Jessie	8		
Reeves	Isaac	52	Wiltshire	Farm Labourer
	Mary A.	52		
	Caleb	20	T/F to Single Men	
	Isabella	18	T/F to Single women	Servant
	Emily	10		
Whiting	Isaac	43	Oxon	Farm Labourer
	Emma	35		
	Mary A.	25	T/F Single women	Servant
	Martha	19	T/F Single women	Servant
Collins	Michael	37	Clare	Farm Labourer
	Bridget	27		
	Martin	5		
	Richard	3		
Single Men				
Farrell	Eugene	20	Kerry	Servant
Conniham	John	22	Kerry	Labourer
Cumming	William	22	Wigtonshire	Shepherd
Cumming	Andrew	27	Wigtonshire	Shepherd
Conners	William	22	Limerick	Carpenter
Conners	David	21	Limerick	Carpenter
Fenton	Michael	23	Limerick	Labourer
Foley	Timothy	22	Kerry	Labourer
Gleeson	Patrick	30	Tipperary	Ploughman
Holman	J. Small	22	Devon	Gc. Labourer
Hill	John	27	Cambridge	Signalman
Kinsley	Joseph	27	Dublin	Shoemaker
Martin	Matthew	26	Limerick	Farm Labourer
McNeill	John	20	Derry	Labourer
McGrath	John	21	Tipperary	Farm Labourer
Norton	John	19	Leicestershire	Brickmaker
Newton	George	17	Middlesex	Labourer

Passenger Lists

Penfold	Richard	24	Surrey	Compositor
Penfold	Ann	45	T/F Single women	Nurse
Penfold	Emily	19	T/F Single women	
Penfold	Walter W.	10		
Quick	John	19	Kerry	Labourer
Riddle	Thomas W.	22	Kerry	Labourer
Blake	Henry	23	Wiltshire	Currier
Callanan	James	21	Galway	Labourer
Collin	Ralph	27	Durham	Blacksmith
Diver	Richard	21	Donegal	Farm Labourer
Elsom	Edward	33	Cambridge	Labourer
Hunt	Frank	22	Wiltshire	Mason
Jauncy	Henry	21	Middlesex	Smith
Jones	William	21	Limerick	Labourer
Keenan	Michael	21	Westmeath	Farm Labourer
Lien	Michael	18	Kerry	Labourer
Magher	Anthony	32	Limerick	Farm Labourer
Murphy	Lawrence	22	Limerick	Labourer
Walsh	William	24	Waterford	Labourer
Hunt	Edward	30	Wiltshire	Farm Labourer
Hunt	James	26	Wiltshire	Gardener
Hogan	Matthew	21	Clare	Gad
Lien	Patrick	20	Kerry	Labourer
McIver	Mundo	23	Rofs??	Shepherd
Matheson	Roderick	21	Rofs??	Shepherd
Duck	Stephen	26	Berkshire	Stoker
McEwan	David	26	Devon	Labourer
Wallington	Edmund	18	Kent	Labourer
O'Connell	James	21	Limerick	Ploughman
Campbell	J.W.L.	20	Sussex	Printer
Brocklebank	William	21	Cheshire	Joiner
Spencer	Edward	36	Lancashire	Farmer
Spencer	William E.	11		
Houngan	Terence	26	Tipperary	Labourer
Crowe	Timothy	22	Tipperary	Labourer
Leen	Patrick	21	Kerry	Labourer
Leen	Catherine	17	T/F to Single Women	Dairymaid
Brien	James	26	Kerry	Labourer
Fitzgerald	Ganett	25	Kerry	Labourer
O'Connell	Patrick	19	Limerick	Ploughman
Single Women				
Baker	Alice	19	Herts	Housmaid
Connolly	Mary	25	Dublin	Saleswomen
Dowling	Catherine	23	Limerick	Housemaid
English	Sarah N.	26	Cornwall	Cook
Hadler	Mary	25	Middlesex	Dressmaker
Hadler	Ann	27	Middlesex	Milliner
Lacey	Hannah	22	Middlesex	Cook
Rainey	Margaret	23	Derry	Housemaid
Rooney	Mary J.	22	Fermanagh	Servant
Storey	Lizzie	15	Fermanagh	Nursemaid

		1/2		
Sharp	Ada	17	Glamorganshire	Servant
Taylor	Mary	24	Clare	Servant
McGrane	Eliza	17	Dublin	Servant
McGrath	Ellen	24	Limerick	Dairymaid
Vaughan	Honora	22	Cork	Servant
Snelgrove	Jane	22	Lancashire	Housemaid
Bryant	Rachael	28	Middlesex	Servant
Frances	Mary	20	Galway	Servant
Lawless	Bridget	19	Galway	Servant
Frances	Honor	17	Galway	Servant
Flannery	Bridget	19	Clare	Servant
Reidy	Catherine	18	Kerry	Dairymaid
Rogerson	Mrs C.	35	Dublin	Matron on board ship
McQuinn	Honorah	21	Kerry	Housemaid
Nicholl	Mary	35	Wexford	Cook
Flahue	Margaret	33	Kerry	Servant
Flahue	Maurice	14	T/F single Men	
McGiverin	Mary	18	Roscommon	Servant
McGiverin	Jane	16	Roscommon	Servant
Shanahan	Ellen	21	Tipperary	Servant

1876

London 16 June 1876 – Wellington 18 September 1876

Name		Age	County	Occupation
Chief cabin passengers				
Campbell	W.D.			
Croker	Mr.			
Lindsay	Reverend J.			
	Miss			
Peat	Mr D.			
	Jane			
	Jane			
Rive	P. A.			
Shaw	J. W.			
Young	J. E.			
Second cabin passengers				
Allan	Mr.			
Bristand	P.			
Franklin	Mr. J.			
	Margaret			
	John A.			
Gray	Mr. J.			

	Caroline			
Hill	S. C.			
	H.			
Smith	Miss			
	Miss C.			
Steerage passengers				
Adams	H. J.			
Coleman	J. W.			
Eaves	J.			
Glacken	D.			
Milhan	W.			
Perry	J.			
Thompson	J.			
	E. H.			
Twistleton	H. j.			
Whisker	J.			

1877

London 4 June 1877 – Wellington 26 October 1877

Name	
Saloon passengers	
Braddick	Mr.
Burraud	Mr. C. D. and family (5)
Clarkson	Miss
Dewes	Mr.
Empson	Mr.
Hutchison	Mr.
Southwell	Mr.
Young	Mr. W. and family (3)
Second Cabin	
Best	Miss
Blake	Mr. (3)
Davis	Mr.
French	Mr.
Grant	Mr.
McCutchan	Mr.

McCutchan	Mr. and family (10)			
Rogers	Mr.			
Sproulo	Mr.			
Turley	Mrs.			
Steerage				
Brise	Mr.			
Brown	Mr.			
Deacon	Mr.			
Fraser	Mr. and Mrs.			
Mason	Mr. and family (7)			
Smaller	Mrs.			
Smaller	Mr. (3)			

1878

London 30 May 1878 – Wellington 28 August 1878

Name		Age	County	Occupation
Saloon passengers				
Brookman	Mr J. G.			
	Mrs.			
	Howden			
	Ethel			
Clarke	E. F.			
Clifford	William			
Cragg	J. C.			
Mallinson	T.			
Philcox	A.			
Sperry	J.			
Second cabin passengers				
Hopkins	Charles			
Johnston	J.			
Joseph	D. T.			
Kennerley	Joseph			
	H. B.			
	Elizabeth C.			
	Thomas			
Logan	Francis			
Morris	T.			

Peach	Comyers				
	Ann				
	Frances				
	Comyers				
	Constance				
Raven	H. S.				
Tankard	Arthur				
Trischler	Annie				
	Norah				
Smith	L. S.				
Steerage passengers					
Hume	W. H. B.				
Keene	M.				
Kirwin	Miss.				
Marshall	William				
	Catherine G.				
	Elizabeth M				
McKinley	Mr.				
	Mrs.				
	Miss.				
	Dinas				
	Infant daughter				Born on board
Phair	J. C.				
Phale	Patrick				
Smith	A. E.				
Webb	James				
Whitson	A.				

1879

London 7 July 1879 – Wellington 19 October 1879

Name		Age	County	Occupation
Families and children				
Algie	William s	26	Tyrone	Farm labourer
	Mary e	24		
	John	5 months		
Askew	Jonathan	28	Hunts	Farm labourer
	Mary	27		
	Annie	8		

Passenger Lists

	Jonathan	6		
	Laura	3		
Boyden	William	26	Staffordshire	Farm labourer
	Elizabrth a	26		
	John w	6		
	Zachariah	4		
	Jane	1		
Burke	Laurence	36	Tipperary	Farm labourer
	Bridget	35		
	Honora	10		
	Daniel	8		
Dillon	John	23	Clare	Farm labourer
	Sarah	20		
Edgecumbe	John	21	Devon	Farm labourer
	Mary a	20		
Exton	Mark	39	Wiltshire	Farm labourer
	Jane	36		
	Rosa	11		
	Walter	9		
Gadsby	William	27	Lincolnshire	Shepherd
	Jane J	25		
	Eliza	7 months		
Glover	George	36	Devon	Farm labourer
	Mary J	33		
	Grace	8		
	Charles	6		
Gray	Alexander	37	Ross	Farm labourer
	Frances	36		
Griffin	Thomas	60	Armagh	Handloom weaver
	Grace	59		
Hobbs	Ephraim	38	Somerset	Farm labourer
	Jane	29		
	Ephraim	4		
	Charles	2		
Huxtable	James	41	Devon	Farm labourer
	Emma	32		
	Lavinia	11		
	Richard	5		
Locke	Maurice	35	Cork	Farm labourer
	Mary	25		
	Ellen	5		

Passenger Lists

	James	3		
	Mary	1		
Mccloshey	Charles	21	Tyrone	Farm labourer
	Ellen	21		
	Sarah j	1 mth		
Mccrossin	William	24	Tyrone	Farm labourer
	Mary	23		
	Mary a	2		
Mcglinchey	Robert	28	Tyrone	Farm labourer
	Eleanor	29		
	John	2		
Martin	Mark	32	Durham	Farm labourer
	Eliza	32		
	Jane	12		
	John	9		
	Sarah M	7		
	Hannah M	3		
Matthews	John	45	Armagh	Labourer
	Ann	44		
	Thomas J	9		
Moore	George	35	Somerset	Farm labourer
	Mary	32		
	George	5		
Morley	Isaac	26	Yorkshire	Farm labourer
	Sarah A	20		
O'shea	Daniel	35	Yorkshire	Farm labourer
	Johanna	30		
	Mary	17		
	Ellen	16		
	Margaret	15		
	Bridget	14		
Colonial nominated families & children				
Akerman(n)	Henry	38	Dorset	Farm labourer
	Susan	36		
	William	14		
	Elizabeth	12		
	Mary	10		
	Alice	7		
	John	4		
	Charles	1		
Buchan	Alexander	25	Aberdeen	Signalman

Passenger Lists

	Jane	32		
Cosford	James	26	Northampton	Tube drainer
	Alice	20		
Cook	William	24	Surrey	Leather dresser
	Catherine	23		
	Henry C	2 months		
Ellery	Thomas	32	Cornwall	Farm labourer
	Agnes	32		
	Mary A	7		
	Ida B	6		
	Agnes	4		
	Alfred	2		
	Arthur	7 months		
Evans	William	41	Glamorgan	Farm labourer
	Mary	35		
	William	7		
	George M	6		
	Catherine	3 months		
Gray	Richard	33	Lincoln	Farmer
	Sarah	43		
	Florence	8		
Griffin	James	38	Ayr	Power loom worker
	Janet	39		
	Jessie	13		
	Mary	11		
	Marion	4		
	Sarah	2		
Harris	Henry	42	Oxon	Carpenter
	Susan	40		
	Eva	17		
	Henry Thomas	15		
	James F	13		
	Laura	11		
Hayes	John	39	Staffordshire	Engine driver
	Mary A	37		
	Charles	9		
	John	7		
	Agnes	5		
	Ellen	7 months		
Hewett	Henry	30	Hants	Mariner
	Sophia A	29		

Passenger Lists

Hobson	Thomas	27	Lancashire	Hatter
	Annie	26		
	Ada	2		
	Gertrude	4 months		
Lee	James	29	Essex	Joiner
	Emma	29		
Naylor	Edward	38	Yorkshire	Blacksmith
	Mary J	36		
	Samuel	15		
	Annie	10		
	Arthur	6		
	Edward	4		
	Agnes	2		
	Harry	3 months		
Paul	Richard	44	Cornwall	Blacksmith
	Elizabeth	43		
	Jane	21		
	Elizabeth	19		
	Joseph	16		
	Caroline	14		
	William	11		
	Isabel	9		
Reise	Gustave	40	Germany	Farm labourer
	Henrietta	41		
Russell	Joseph B	35	Lincolnshire	Labourer
	Annie D	32		
	Edith	13		
	Louisa	10		
Sexton	Edward	38	Middlesex	General labourer
	Emily	38		
	Emily	16		
	Elizabeth	14		
	Louisa	7		
Monal	William	45	Shetland	Farmer
	Grace	42		
	John	22		
	Robert	21		
	Ursula	19		
	Gilbert	17		
	Elizabeth	16		
	Jessie	15		

Passenger Lists

	Ellen	14		
	James	13		
	Mary	12		
	Samuel	10		
	Grace	8		
	Arthur	5		
	Charlotte			
Yonson	Emanuel	29	Sweden	Farm labourer
	Johanna	27		
	John	10		
Single men				
Bale	Alfred	22	Devon	Farm labourer
Breakivall	Charles	39	Shropshire	Farm labourer
Buckingham	Thomas J	25	Cornwall	Farm labourer
Burke	Daniel	19	Tipperary	Farm labourer
	John	17	Tipperary	
	Laurence	14		
Byrne	James	24	Louth	Farm labourer
Casey	Patrick	20	Cork	Carpenter
Clarke	Thomas	20	Caven	Farm labourer
Cloghessey	David	21	Limerick	Farm labourer
Conneely	David	23	Galway	Farm labourer
Corkoran	Charles	23	Kerry	Farm labourer
Doherty	Matthew	23	Tipperary	Farm labourer
Dwyer	Pat	22	Tipperary	Farm labourer
Farrell	Loughlin	24	Cavan	Farm labourer
Foster	Richard	15	Devon	Farm labourer
Gallacher	Robert	21	Dumbarton	Farm labourer
Griffin	James	20	Waterford	Farm labourer
Gwilliam	Llewellyn	19	Wiltshire	Farm labourer
Ham	Job	44	Devon	Farm labourer
Ham	William	18	Cornwall	Farm labourer
Harris	Francis	21	Somerset	Farm labourer
Hawkey	William M	21	Cornwall	
Hogg	John	22	Roxburgh	Farm labourer
Hurley	Jeremiah	24	Limerick	
Johnson	James	32	Shetland	Farm labourer
Keeffe	Denis	17	Cork	Farm labourer
Kelcher	Pat	18	Cork	Farm labourer
Kelly	Thomas	23	Tyrone	Farm labourer
Kiely	Michael	21	Cork	Farm labourer

Passenger Lists

Lang	James	23	Lanarkshire	Farm labourer
Liddy	James	22	Cork	Farm labourer
Lydon	Martin	21	Galway	Farm labourer
Mcelroy	Owen	19	Dublin	Farm labourer
Mckenzie	Francis	21	Caithness	Shepherd
Mcmahon	Patrick	24	Clare	Farm labourer
Maher	Michael	22	Limerick	Farm labourer
Mannagh	Aleander	21	Tyrone	Farm labourer
Mason	Samuel	22	Cheshire	Farm labourer
	Henry	20	Cheshire	Farm labourer
Moher	Michael	19	Cork	Farm labourer
Montague	James	23	Tyrone	Farm labourer
Moore	William	24	Cheshire	Engine driver
Murphy	John	22	Cork	Farm labourer
Nocklon	William	21	Galway	Farm labourer
O'Neill	John	22	Kerry	Farm labourer
O'Sullivan	Daniel	20	Cork	Farm labourer
	Florence	22	Cork	Farm labourer
O'Sulliavan	Timothy	22	Kerry	Farm labourer
Patton	Christopher	19	Kerry	Farm labourer
Riordom	John	22	Tipperary	Farm labourer
Rutledge	Michael	20	Galway	Farm labourer
Ryan	James	20	Tipperary	Farm labourer
	Jeremiah	20	Tipperary	Farm labourer
Saunders	James	26	Devon	Farm labourer
Savage	Patrick	25	Kerry	Farm labourer
	Jeremiah	21	Kerry	Farm labourer
Smith	Harry	18	Northampton	Farm labourer
Smith	James	21	Shetland	Farm labourer
Sweeney	Timothy	23	Limerick	Farm labourer
Walsh	Martin	25	Galway	Farm labourer
Walsh	Patrick	23	Waterford	Farm labourer
Colonial nominated single men				
Bush	Robert	21	Middlesex	Fitter
Carrel	John c	24	Jersey	Plumber
Farrell	Michael	23	Clare	Farm labourer
Fitzgerald	Thomas	23	Kerry	Farm labourer
Foley	Michael	24	Kerry	Farm labourer
Ling	Henry	18	Surrey	Painter
Lloyd	John E	22	Shropshire	Barman
Mcmanns	John	20	Roscommon	Farm labourer

Madigan	Martin	30	Limerick	Farm labourer
	James	19	Limerick	Farm labourer
O'Brien	Timothy	20	Kerry	Farm labourer
	William	24	Kerry	Farm labourer
	Mary	18	Kerry	Dairymaid
	Ellen	18	Kerry	Dairymaid
O'Driscoll	Micheal	20	Cork	Farm labourer
	James	20	Cork	Farm labourer
Powell	George	26	Limerick	Labourer
	Bridget	22	Limerick	Servant
Rankin	John	32	Lanarkshire	Labourer - New Plymouth
Smith	Thomas	30	Middlesex	Labourer
Sullivan	John	20	Kerry	Farm labourer
Tobyn	Richard	21	Roscommon	Farm labourer
	Mary	17	Roscommon	General servant
Twomey	Denis	22	Cork	General labourer
Williams	Robert	29	Middlesex	Dealer in waste paper
Single women				
Allen	Margaret	18	Antrim	General servant
Barnes	Emily B	24	Dorset	Housemaid
Bird	Hannah	24	Cork	General servant
Bradley	Martha E	20	Lincolnshire	Cook
Burke	Mary	18	Tipperary	Servant
	Annie	15	Tipperary	Servant
	Bridget	12	Tipperary	
Campbell	Mary	25	Monaghan	General servant
Caslin	Bridget	24	Roscommon	General servant
Clarke	Rose A	20	Monaghan	General servant
Coveney	Sarah	19	Waterford	Housemaid
Donnelly	Elizabeth	20	Lanarkshire	General servant
Emery	Edith J	22	Essex	Housemaid
Evans	Ellen	22	Kerry	Dairymaid
Flynn	Kate	20	Limerick	General servant
Fraser	Mary	27	Shetland	Housemaid
Griffin	Sarah	16	Lanarkshire	Power loom weaver
Hancock	Elizabeth	26	Somersetshire	Cook
Jacob	Martha	16	Donegal	General servant
James	Elizabeth A	21	Cornwall	General servant
Keenan	Catherine	20	Monaghan	General servant
	Mary	18	Monaghan	General servant
Kirby	Mary	24	Monaghan	General servant

Langhland	Agnes	25	Lanarkshire	General servant
Lee	Catherine	19	Galway	Nurse
Mckenzie	Catherine	25	Rosshire	General servant
Mannagh	Ellen	23	Tyrone	General servant
	Mary	20	Tyrone	General servant
Marron	Mary	18	Sligo	Housemaid
Marshall	Margaret	19	Tyrone	Housemaid
Moffat	Cecilia	22	Northumberland	General servant
Rankin	Mary	60	Aryshire	
Real	Honora	22	Northumberland	General servant
Real	Mary	23	Limerick	General servant
Robertson	Agnes	19	Shetland	Housemaid
Robertson	Lydia	17	Middlesex	General servant
Salter	Mary A	33	Montgomery	Housemaid
Semple	Martha J	22	Tyrone	General servant
Sinclair	Elizabeth	26	Shetland	General servant
Sullivan	Julia	22	Kerry	Housemaid
Sweeney	Mary	21	Kerry	General servant
Tarran	Isabella	40	Yorkshire	Housekeeper
	John J	15	Yorkshire	Farm labourer
Thornton	Mary	19	Galway	General servant
Twatt	Jemima	20	Shetland	Cook
Walsh	Maria	23	Kilkenny	Housemaid
Wright	Lizzie	21	Antrim	Nurse
Colonial nominated single women				
Baumler	Mary	28	Germany	Dressmaker
	Amelia O	5		
Cole	Elizabeth	20	Middlesex	General servant
Downey	Hannah	18	Kerry	General servant
Foley	Mary	20	Kerry	Dairymaid
Jorgensen	Johanna M	24	Denmark	Servant by calling
Larson	Wilhelmina	22	Denmark	Servant
Frame	Grace	60	Lanark	
	William	24	Lanark	Patternmaker
	David	16	Lanark	Architect
Galway	Ellen	18	Kerry	General servant
Gnatt	Eva	60	Germany	
Glynn	Catherine	18	Roscommon	Housemaid
Hamilton	Jean	33	Ayrshire	Milkwoman New Plymouth
	Mary	11		
	Margaret	7		

		James	4		
		Sarah J	3		
Hanson		Johanna	54	Sweden	
Keating		Johanna	17	Limerick	General servant
Madigan		Ellen	29	Limerick	General servant
Mahoney		Mary A	24	Limerick	General servant
		Ellen	22	Limerick	General servant
Mathew		Elizabeth	23	Armagh	Cook
Moore		Mary	20	Tipperary	General servant
Morgan		Ann E	34	Middlesex	Dressmaker
		Ann	8		
Rankin		Margaret	34	Ayrshire	General servant New Plymouth
Skinner		Catherine	25	Middlesex	Nurse
Summers		Rosina	18	Middlesex	Upholsterer
Yonson		Christina	21	Sweden	General servant

1880

London 20 July 1880 – Port Chalmers 21 October 1880

Saloon	
Chief Cabin	
Allardyce	Mr. A. C.
Bamford	Mr. H. W.
Martin	Mr. A. R.
Quiche	Mr. E.
Second Cabin and Steerage	
Bayfield	Mr.
Bragg	Mr.
Greenless	Mr.
Hay	Miss.
Holshan	Mr.
Manley	Mr. and Mrs.
Mark	Mr.
Maxwell	Mr.
Moore	Mr. and Mrs.
Patillo	Mr. H.
Paton	Mr.
Sharp	Mr. and Mrs. and

	child
Sharp	Mr.
Spence	Mrs. and child
Stanley	Mr.
Whittingham	Mr. and Mrs. and 2 children
Wilson	Mr. and Mrs. and 4 children
Young	Mr.

1881

London 5 June 1881 – Auckland 28 September 1881

Name		Age	County	Occupation
Chief cabin passengers				
Brown	Edward			
	Mrs.			
	John			
	Herbert			
Goodwyn	Miss F. A.			
Magels	Miss S.			
Oddie	A. R.			
Peake	H. S.			Listed in both 1st & 2nd cabin
Porter	H. M.			
Rygate	Dr			Surgeon on board
Second cabin passengers				
Allwood	A. F.			
Beaumont	M			
	L. B.			
Blyth	Samuel			
Edwards	E. H.			
	Mrs.			
Hands	Frederick			
Le Feaux	W.			
Mayers	G. R.			
Peake	H. S.			Listed in both 1st & 2nd cabin
Robinson				
Smith	T. R.			
	Mary			
	Edith			

Passenger Lists

	Lilian			
Verner	F.			
	Mrs			
Steerage passengers				
Adams	James			
	Hannah			
	James			
	Robert			
	Samuel			
	Thomas			
Archibald	Robert			
Bell	Robert			
Carter	W. H.			
	Susan			
	Alice			
	Emily			
	Hannah			
	William			
	Lucy			
Carter	Mary			
	Charles			
Clifton	William			
Cook	Henrietta			
	Annie			
Goodley	Catherine			
	Joseph			
	George			
Hough	John			
Laver	Robert			
	Mercy			
	Maria			
	Henry			
	Ellen			
	Charles			
Nicholson	Mr.			
	Mrs.			
	Flora			
	Donald			
	Margaret			
Patterson	Mrs.			
	William			

Sage	George	
	Agnes	
	John	
	Mary	
	Agnes	
Shackleton	J. M.	
	Mary	
	Catherine	
Thompson	Robert	
Williams	John	
	Mrs.	
	Miss S.	
	Miss K.	
	Miss M.	
	Miss K.	
	Thomas	
Wood	Joseph	
	Mary	

1882

London 9 July 1882 – Port Chalmers 10 October 1882

Name	
Saloon passengers	
West	Mr. A. B.
Noel-Smith	Mr
Steerage	
Richardson	Mr
Richardson	Mrs
Richardson	Family (3)
Brailey	Mr
Brailey	Mrs
Brailey	Family (2)
Varry	Mrs
Chappell	Mrs
Fletcher	Miss
Prain	Miss
Boder	Miss
Mackay	Miss

Mason	Mr
Steilberg	Mr
Lowenstern	Mr
Whitaker	Mr
Gibbs	Mr

1883

London 2 June 1883 - Auckland 6 September 1883

Name		Age	County	Occupation
Saloon passengers				
Blandpied	George			
	George			
Ling	W. P.			
Thomas	Frank			
Webbe	W. H.			
Second cabin passengers				
Halford	Ellen			
	Florence E.			
Menzies	David			
	Helen			
	Margaret			
	J.			
Steerage passengers				
Adamson	J. W.			
	Sabina			
	Madelina			
	Percy			
	Thomas			
Broomfield	Henry			
Clarke	William			
	Mary			
	William A.			
Gellender	Walter C.			
Gordon	Michael			
Janvein	Percy			
	L.			
Jones	Albert W.			
	Jane			

	Ruth E.			
	Rosa F.			
Lee	Moses			
Matthews	William			
McCartney	Charles			
	Mary			
	Florence			
	Charles			
Mickle	David			
Miller	James			
	Isabella			
	James			
	Katherine			
	Isabella			
Rogers	W. J.			
Stafford	Henry			
	Annie			
	Susanna			

1884

London 16 April 1884 – Wellington 18 July 1884

Name	
Saloon passengers	
England	Richard
Flux	Mr. and Mrs. G. and child
Fletcher	A.
Clarke	F.
Lodge	Charles
Second Cabin	
Seymour	Miss Ruth
Seymour	Miss Mary
Bridge	Mr. and Mrs. and 2 sons
Welch	Mr. and Mrs.
Matthews	Mr. and Mrs.
Ashton	Diana
Moody	Harry
Carter	John

Third Cabin	
Clarke	Mr. and Mrs. J. and child
Cousins	Mr. and Mrs. Robert
Gurney	Mrs. and family (4)
Bryce	Mr. and Mrs. Peter
Hutchison	Mr. and Mrs. and 2 children
Holyman	Joseph
Board	James
Slade	Hugh
Fear	John
Davidson	Walter
Rea	Joseph
Gunn	Thomas
Wigham	M.[43]

1885

London 16 June 1885 – Wellington 29 September 1885

Name		Age	County	Occupation
Saloon passengers				
Atkens	Miss			
Heath	Miss			
	Miss L.			
Olny	Miss			
Ward	Miss			
Second cabin passengers				
Fredwell	Mr.			
Kelson	Mr.			
Shield	Mr.			
Steerage passengers				
12 in steerage[44]				

1887

London 24 July 1887 – Auckland 8 November 1887

Name	
Second Cabin	
Weldon	Mr. (4)
Dunn	Mr.
Third Cabin	
Bird	Mr.
Wilcox	Mr.
Dougherty	Mr.
Cobern	Mr.[4]

1888

London 8 August 1888 – Auckland 7 December 1888

Name	
Latham	Miss.
Latham	Mr. J.
Latham	Mr. H.
Latham	Mr. J.
Wyatt	H. S.
Croft	
Broadbent	C. H.
Pilkington	E. L.
Groves	L. C.
Cookson	Mr and Mrs. R.
Maule	Miss.
Dredge	Miss
Shepherd	Miss
Rockstro	Mr. C.
Gunning	Mr. J.
Osborne	Mr. Chas.
Howell	Mr. Chas.
Macklin	Mr. E. J.
Emlis	Mr J.
Harvey	Mr. C.[28]

1889

London 15 June 1889 – Wellington 15 September 1889

Name	
Londown	Mr.
Matthei	Mr.
England	Mr.[29]

1890

London 31 May 1890 – Auckland 17 September 1890

Name	
Phillips	Miss
Phillips	Miss[45]

1894

Liverpool 4 September 1894 – Wellington 11 December 1894

Name	
Meredith	Mr. (shipping clerk of Gracie Beazley & Co. Liverpool.)
Meredith	Mrs.
Watts	Miss (sister-in-law of Mr. Meredith)[34]

1897

London 29 May 1897 – Bluff 10 September 1897

Name[46]	
Beaumont	G. H. (1st Mate)
Heron	Thomas (2nd Mate)
Sreppey	Jonathan S. (3rd

	Mate)
Coull	George (Carpenter)
Windlaw	Jonathan (Sails & A.B.)
Young	William (Steward)
Rundle	Jonathan W. (A.B.)
Andersen	Jonathan (A.B.)
Olsen	D. (A.B.)
Hennessy	James (A.B.)
Lindson	W. (A.B.)
Andersen	C. (A.B.)
Saunel	A. (A.B.)
Jeffery	A. (A.B.)
Rellett	James (A.B.)
Wright	H. S. (A.B.)
Hilton	A. N. (Apprentice)
Garrett	C. C. (Apprentice)
Gardiner	R. M. (Apprentice)
Sowals	E. D. (Apprentice)
~~Broughton~~	~~B. D. (Apprentice)~~
Welsh	S. R. (Apprentice)

1899

London 29 June 1899 – Bluff 4 October 1899

Name[47]	
Beaumont	G. H. (1st Mate)
Garrett	C. G. (2nd Mate)
Fold	A. W. (3rd Mate)
Coull	George (Carpenter)
Young	William (Steward)
Watkins	J. S. (Cook)
Windland	Jonathan (A. B. & Sails)
Chambell	W. G. (A. B.)
Salker	H. (A.B.)
Leners	C. (A. B.)
Farrell	F. (A. B.)
Jones	B. (A. B.)

Passenger Lists

Wilson	I. J. (A.B.)
Foley	J. (A. B.)
Shackson	R. (A. B.)
Fristran	G. (A. B.)
Hoerop	William (A. B.)
Adeif	B. D. (A. B.)
Broughton	R. D. (Apprentice)
Barrow	R. M. (Apprentice)
Philpott	Charles (Apprentice)
Briegers	? A. (Apprentice)
Wiliams	W. W. (Apprentice)
Leddes	Henry H. B. (Apprentice)

References

1. Loss Of The Ship Blue Jacket By Fire. 5 June 1869. *Press* 2 (1869).
2. Tales Of Adventure. Captain Henry Rose. 23 June 1923. *Auckl. Star* 24 (1923).
3. Arrival Of The Zealandia. Journey Summary and cabin passengers. 8 November 1887. *Auckl. Star* 4 (1887).
4. Shipping Telegrams. Zealandia journey summary. 6 January 1873. *Otago Dly. Times* 2 (1873).
5. Shipping. Biography of Captain Ruth. 16 September 1889. *Dly. Telegr.* 2 (1889).
6. Rotoroa Island. *Wikipedia Free Encycl.* (2013). at <http://en.wikipedia.org/w/index.php?title=Rotoroa_Island&oldid=544468654>
7. Taonga, N. Z. M. for C. and H. T. M. Settlement in the provinces: 1853 to 1870. at <http://www.teara.govt.nz/en/history-of-immigration/5>
8. Shaw, Savill And Albion Company | NZETC. at <http://nzetc.victoria.ac.nz/tm/scholarly/tei-Bre01Whit-t1-body-d5.html>
9. Acland, J. B. A. Shipping papers 'Clontarf, A1': ships regulations and plan. University of Canterbury. Acland. (1855).
10. Costs and Wages in Great Britain. at <http://www.rootsweb.ancestry.com/~irlcar2/wages.htm>
11. Purdy, F. On the Earnings of Agricultural Labourers in England and Wales, 1860. *J. Stat. Soc. Lond.* **24,** 328–373 (1861).
12. Life at Sea: Museum Victoria. at <http://museumvictoria.com.au/discoverycentre/websites-mini/journeys-australia/1850s70s/life-at-sea/>
13. Leininger Geschichtsblätter. Published Germany, 1910. Translated by Klaus Nasterlack, 2012. (1910).
14. Shaw, Savill and Co. at <http://www.merchantnavyofficers.com/shawsavill.html>
15. Arrival Of The Ship Zealandia. Journey summary. 22 November 1869. *Press* 2 (1869).
16. Arrival Of The Ship Zealandia. Journey summary. 24 December 1870. *Star* 2 (1870).
17. Diary of Edward Evans while on board the 'Zealandia' (ship) - The 'Zealandia' (ship) departed from Gravesend on 23 September 1870 arrived at Lyttelton on 23 December 1870 (R20351920). Agency ACHU. Series 19357. Record Group, MISC63. Box/Item 1/. at <http://www.archway.archives.govt.nz/ViewFullItem.do?code=20351920>
18. Arrival Of The Ship Zealandia From London. 11 December 1871. *Press* 2 (1871).
19. Arrival Of The Zealandia. Journey Summary. 1 December 1873. *Otago Dly. Times* 2 (1873).
20. Arrival Of The Zealandia. Journey summary and cabin passengers. 16 October 1874. *Auckl. Star* 2 (1874).
21. Shipping. Arrival of the Zealandia. Includes journey summary and passenger list for cabin passengers. 11 October 1882. *Otago Dly. Times* 2 (1882).
22. Arrival Of The Zealandia. 6 September 1883. *Auckl. Star* 2 (1883).
23. Saltwater Yarns. Captain Ruth. 4 March 1908. *Auckl. Star* 6 (1908).
24. Arrival Of The Ship Zealandia. Mentions 25 passengers but not by name. 18 October 1886. *Press* 2 (1886).
25. Telegrams. Zealandia brings 35 passengers. 18 October 1886. *Thames Star* 2 (1886).
26. Shipping. Arrival of the Zealandia. Cabin passengers and journey summary. 8 December 1888. *N. Z. Her.* 4 (1888).
27. Page 2 Advertisements Column 1. Zealandia summary. 18 September 1889. *Wanganui Her.* 2 (1889).
28. The Ship Zealandia. Journey Summary. 18 September 1890. *Auckl. Star* 4 (1890).
29. The Ship Zealandia. Journey Summary. 11 August 1891. *Star* 2 (1891).
30. Arrival Of The Zealandia. Journey Summary. 3 August 1892. *Otago Dly. Times* 1 (1892).
31. By Telegraph. The journey summary for the Zealandia. 7 October 1893. *Evening Post* 2 (1893).
32. Evening Post. Wednesday, December 12, 1894. One passenger mentioned by the Zealandia. *Evening Post* 2 (1894).
33. Arrival Of The Zealandia. Journey summary. 28 November 1895. *Otago Witn.* 42 (1895).
34. Shipping. Zealandia arrived. 11 September 1897. *Otago Dly. Times* 1 (1897).
35. The Zealandia | NZETC. at <http://nzetc.victoria.ac.nz/tm/scholarly/tei-Bre01Whit-t1-body-d44.html>

36. Southland News Notes. Zealandia arrival. 29 September 1898. *Otago Witn.* 31 (1898).
37. The Ship Zealandia. Full summary of journey to Nelson. 15 January 1901. *Nelson Evening Mail* 2 (1901).
38. Ship Zealandia 18 December 1901. *Nelson Evening Mail* 2 (1901).
39. Sailed. Ship Zealandia for the Bluff. 14 January 1902. *Nelson Evening Mail* 2 (1902).
40. Sailed. Zealandia for London with bales of wool. 1 March 1902. *Nelson Evening Mail* 2 (1902).
41. *The story of the Diver Family, From County Donegal to North Otago. By W. Ray Dobson (Diver Trust).*
42. *The Voyages of the Zealandia, which bought Richard Diver And Catherine Hegarty to New Zealand in 1875. By W. Ray Dobson.*
43. Arrival Of The Ship Zealandia, From London. Short journey summary and cabin passenger list. 18 July 1884. *Evening Post* 2 (1884).
44. Telegraphic Shipping. Zealandia 106 days from London. 30 September 1885. *Auckl. Star* 2 (1885).
45. Arrivals. Zealandia cabin passengers. 18 September 1890. *Auckl. Star* 4 (1890).
46. New Zealand, Archives New Zealand, Passenger Lists, 1839-1973 Image New Zealand, Archives New Zealand, Passenger Lists, 1839-1973; pal:/MM9.3.1/TH-267-12698-2736-50 — FamilySearch.org. Crew List 1897. at <https://familysearch.org/pal:/MM9.3.1/TH-267-12698-2736-50?cc=1609792&wc=MP7B-LLK:119037201,119067701,119178901>
47. New Zealand, Archives New Zealand, Passenger Lists, 1839-1973 Image New Zealand, Archives New Zealand, Passenger Lists, 1839-1973; pal:/MM9.3.1/TH-266-12440-14895-57 — FamilySearch.org. Crew List 1899. at <https://familysearch.org/pal:/MM9.3.1/TH-266-12440-14895-57?cc=1609792&wc=MP7L-HZT:119037201,119030702,119178901>

www.ingramcontent.com/pod-product-compliance
Lightning Source LLC
Chambersburg PA
CBHW050647160426
43194CB00010B/1836